GENDER, ATHLETES' RIGHTS, AND THE COURT OF ARBITRATION FOR SPORT

GENDER, ATHLETES' RIGHTS, AND THE COURT OF ARBITRATION FOR SPORT

BY

HELEN JEFFERSON LENSKYJ
University of Toronto, Canada

United Kingdom — North America — Japan
India — Malaysia — China

Emerald Publishing Limited
Howard House, Wagon Lane, Bingley BD16 1WA, UK

First edition 2018

British Library Cataloguing in Publication Data
A catalogue record for this book is available from the British
Library

ISBN: 978-1-78754-240-2 (Print)
ISBN: 978-1-78743-753-1 (Online)
ISBN: 978-1-78743-969-6 (Epub)

Printed and bound by CPI Group (UK) Ltd, Croydon, CR0 4YY

ISOQAR certified
Management System,
awarded to Emerald
for adherence to
Environmental
standard
ISO 14001:2004.

Certificate Number 1985
ISO 14001

INVESTOR IN PEOPLE

ACKNOWLEDGEMENTS

Thanks to social media, a Twitter post several years ago first drew my attention to the potential shortcomings of the Court of Arbitration for Sport (CAS). Following up on comments praising CAS decisions, this post raised a key question: has justice been sacrificed in the interests of speed and efficiency? And so, when my colleague Stephen Wagg invited me to contribute to the *Journal of Criminological Research Policy and Practice* special issue on sport, crime and deviance, I started researching sport exceptionalism, sports law, and CAS. I soon discovered that these topics warranted deeper investigation, resulting in this book. Coincidentally, around the same time, Stephen Wagg and Philippa Grand, Publisher and Head of Social Sciences, Emerald Group Publishing had been discussing a possible book series on gender and sport. I now have the privilege of editing this series, together with a team of accomplished sport scholars, and I am delighted that this volume is the first publication in the series.

Conversations about these issues, online and/or in person, with colleagues and friends Daryl Adair, Janaka Biyanwila, Andrew Byrnes, Nikki Dryden, Janice Forsyth, Kevin Lindgren, Jason Mazanov, Stephen Wagg, Kristen Worley, and many others were invaluable, as were the comments from anonymous reviewers. I am also grateful to the small but growing number of legal scholars, sports lawyers, sociologists, historians, and scientists who have critically examined issues of athletes' rights and sports law, and whose work has inspired this project. Thanks to Philippa Grand, Rachel Ward, and the editorial team at Emerald Publishing for their commitment to the project. My partner Liz Green provided her usual valuable feedback and expert proofreading. As always, I thank Liz and my children for their love and support.

Note: An earlier version of some sections of the book appeared in the article 'Sport exceptionalism and the Court of Arbitration for Sport', *Journal of Criminological Research Policy and Practice* 4(1), 2018, 5−17.

CONTENTS

LIST OF ABBREVIATIONS

ABP	Athlete Biological Passport
ADR	Alternate Dispute Resolution
AHD	Ad Hoc Division
AIS	androgen insensitivity syndrome
AOC	Australian Olympic Committee
ASADA	Australian Sports Anti-Doping Authority
BOA	British Olympic Association
CAS	Court of Arbitration for Sport
CCES	Canadian Centre for Ethics in Sport
DSD	disorders of sexual development
EC	European Commission
ECHR	European Convention on Human Rights
ECJ	European Court of Justice
FEI	Fédération Equestre Internationale (equestrian)
FIFA	Fédération Internationale de Football Association
FIG	Fédération Internationale de Gymnastique
FINA	Fédération Internationale de Natation (swimming)
FIS	Fédération Internationale de Ski
FISA	International Rowing Federation
FIVB	Fédération International de Volleyball
HRTO	Human Rights Tribunal of Ontario

IAAF	International Association of Athletics Federations
ICAS	International Council of Arbitration for Sport
ICF	International Canoe Federation
IF	international federation
IOC	International Olympic Committee
IPC	International Paralympic Committee
ISLJ	International Sports Law Centre
ISU	International Skating Union
ITA	Independent Testing Authority
IWF	International Weightlifting Federation
JADCO	Jamaica Anti-Doping Commission
NADO	National Anti-Doping Organizations (Institute of)
NOC	National Olympic Committee
OCA	Ontario Cycling Association
OHA	Ontario Hockey Association
PCOS	polycystic ovary syndrome
PILA	Private International Law Act
ROC	Russian Olympic Committee
RUSADA	Russian Anti-Doping Agency
SFT	Swiss Federal Tribunal
SGB	sports governing body
TAS	Tribunal Arbitral du Sport
T/E	testosterone/epistestosterone ratio
TUE	therapeutic use exemption
UCI	Union Cycliste Internationale
UEFA	Union of European Football Associations
UKAD	United Kingdom Anti-Doping

UN	United Nations
USOC	United States Olympic Committee
VANOC	Vancouver Organizing Committee
WADA	World Anti-Doping Agency
WPA	World Players Association

INTRODUCTION

As an activist on gender and sport issues since the early 1980s, I had my first brush with 'the law' in 1986 when I participated as an expert witness in the case of Justine Blainey, a 12-year-old ice hockey player in Toronto, Canada. Blainey had tried out for a boys' team and had qualified, but was barred because the Ontario (men's) Hockey Association (OHA) prohibited girls from playing with boys. The Ontario Women's Hockey Association also objected, predicting that mixed gender teams would signify the end of girls' hockey as we know it. Unfortunately for Blainey, the 1981 Ontario Human Rights Code did not protect the rights of female athletes; Section 19.2 specifically exempted sport/gender complaints.

The legal battles began at the Divisional Court of Ontario, which ruled against Blainey, but in 1986 the Ontario Court of Appeal struck down Section 19.2 on the grounds that it contravened the Canadian Charter of Rights and Freedoms. OHA persevered in an unsuccessful appeal to the Supreme Court of Canada, and, in 1987, the Ontario Human Rights Commission ruled that OHA and Blainey's club had violated the (revised) Code (Vella, 1989). Despite these changes, the last 30 years have seen repeated incidents of discrimination of this kind, mostly involving young female players at the local level. Since 1983, athletes have had access to a specialized sport 'court' that promised to resolve disputes efficiently and fairly. The extent to which the Court of Arbitration for Sport (CAS) has achieved its goal, particularly in cases involving women and members of ethnic minorities, is the subject of this book.

1.1. THE COURT OF ARBITRATION FOR SPORT

The history and functions of CAS have attracted a considerable volume of discussion and debate in law literature, in contrast to the relatively low level of attention these topics have received in sport history, philosophy, or sociology research. There are two important exceptions to this trend — doping and gender testing — which have been the topics of extensive study and critique across the social sciences, exercise sciences, legal studies, and medical science.

In view of the growth of interdisciplinary studies in the academy and the research community since the 1970s, the relative dearth of critique of 'sports law' outside of legal studies is somewhat surprising. Critical scholars do not generally avoid questions of law. For decades, researchers from a range of academic disciplines who focus on gender, sexualities, disability, culture, and 'race'/ethnicity have been tackling legal issues as they apply to the rights and experiences of disadvantaged individuals and groups. Additionally, in western universities, there is a long history of sociologists, social psychologists, historians, and philosophers who are public intellectuals. These scholars collaborate with activists on social justice issues, work that necessarily involves critical analysis of jurisprudence, legislation and law enforcement. 'Sport' and 'law' are socially constructed, and historically and culturally specific, thereby making the concept of 'sports law' a particularly important focus for critical examination.

There are two basic and often unquestioned assumptions that appear in some form or another in most defenses for sports law and a specialized 'sport court': sport is 'big business' and sport is a 'social good.' 'Business' connotes profit – hence the question: who profits? Similarly, on the question of social impacts, who benefits? These are among the basic issues that I address in this book as a sociologist and feminist scholar, but not, I emphasize, as a legal scholar.

Citing the 'big business' argument, a 2013 commentator noted that sport comprised 'more than 3% of world trade and 3.7% of the combined gross national product of the twenty-eight member states of the European Union, comprising some 505 million people' (Blackshaw, 2013, p. 61). However, with the notable exception of football (soccer), which represents almost half of CAS's published cases, many athletes who bring disputes to CAS play sports that contribute little to world trade or GNPs, and the really 'big business' that is American professional sport is outside CAS's jurisdiction. In fact, a case could be made for renaming CAS the 'Court of Arbitration for Football,' and allowing other sport disputes, except for time-sensitive situations occurring at the Olympic Games, to proceed to domestic courts. Regarding the 'big business' rationale, it seems unlikely that any other multinational corporation would be permitted to bypass traditional courts and to choose 'user-friendly and flexible' procedures simply to meet its *special* needs. Yet as the following discussion demonstrates, proponents of sport exceptionalism have successfully promoted the idea that sport's self-regulation and internal dispute resolution procedures are eminently sensible and justified.

1.2. SPORTS LAW: GLOBAL IMPACTS

In my sport-related research and advocacy work since 1980, the focus has mostly been on the 'big picture' – that is, the intersecting impacts of gender, class, 'race'/ethnicity and sexualities on sport and physical activity. It may appear, then, that a narrow focus on the experiences and rights of a relatively small number of high performance athletes should not be my top priority. However, in this book, I will demonstrate that what happens at the highest level of sport has impacts throughout the system. As Mitten and Opie (2012, p. 208) explained in their discussion of evolving sports law, 'the combination of extensive media coverage and strong public interest in sport provides enormous power to convey educational messages to diverse global audiences.' While I continue to identify flaws in 'role model' rhetoric, as I did in my 2012 publication *Gender Politics and the Olympic Industry* and elsewhere, there is no doubt that high performance sport and celebrity athletes have a significant influence, both positive and negative, on children and youth. Mainstream and social media coverage routinely convey idealistic rhetoric aimed at young people – 'follow your dreams... you can be anything you want to be' – but these inspirational messages need to be balanced with realistic warnings that an athlete's life in the fast lane may well prove 'nasty, brutish and short,' as many victims of 'sports law' have experienced.

The consequences of athletes' alleged cheating, misconduct or doping tend to attract as much media attention as their sporting achievements, whether or not these men and women have received fair and just treatment at the hands of sports disciplinary bodies. In fact, with a few recent exceptions – Maria Sharapova and the Russian athletes implicated in doping, for example – CAS itself makes relatively rare appearances in media headlines, but the impacts of CAS decisions shape the lives and livelihoods of countless numbers of aspiring athletes.

An examination of media and public reaction to controversial CAS cases clearly shows how gender, 'race'/ethnicity and other social factors intersect to shape the outcomes: who is demonized? Who gets a second chance? Who is labeled a drug cheat? How do racism and misogyny interact? Which women are disqualified for appearing 'not woman enough'? Which men are excused on the grounds that 'boys will be boys'? Which 'experts' are consulted? Whose voices are silenced? These are among the many 'big picture' issues that I will investigate.

One of the most prolific legal commentators on the topic of CAS is Canadian law professor Richard McLaren, who, in 2016 and 2017, conducted extensive investigations into Russian doping. McLaren has been a CAS arbitrator since 1994, a relevant fact that is generally acknowledged in his own publications but not always noted by authors who cite his work (McLaren, 1998, 2001a, 2001b, 2001c, 2010). Most commentators follow the scholarly convention of disclosing their own personal involvement in CAS cases when contributing to academic journals, and, as in other areas of sports studies, male authors greatly outnumber female. Current or former CAS members who have contributed to the largely positive image of CAS in law literature include Jack Anderson (2000), Michael Beloff (2012), Ian Blackshaw (2003, 2006, 2007), Stefan Netzle (1992), Jan Paulsson (2016), and John Wendt (2012). Similarly, experienced sports lawyers who have represented parties in CAS proceedings have added important commentaries to the law literature, with some taking a more critical stance, including Mark Mangan (2009), Louise Reilly (2012), Antonio Rigozzi, Marjolaine Viret, and Emily Wisnosky (Rigozzi, 2010; Rigozzi, Viret & Wisnosky, 2013, WADC, 2017a, 2017b).

None of these trends are surprising or inappropriate, since arbitrators and sports lawyers would probably not continue their association with CAS if they seriously questioned its underlying premise or its judicial functions. Some of the most incisive critiques of CAS come from relative 'outsiders,' most notably legal scholars, including, among many others, Andrew Byrnes (2016), Antoine Duval (2015, 2016), Hilary Findlay (2013), Ken Foster (2005), and David McArdle (2011, 2013, 2015).

I.3. METHODOLOGY

In terms of primary sources, I have consulted the decisions of CAS and the Swiss Federal Tribunal (SFT), as well as those of other courts, arbitration and disciplinary panels, for the period 1986–2018, with a focus on those cases in which gender and/or 'race'/ethnicity played a part, whether directly or indirectly. Official Olympic industry sources include publications of the IOC, CAS, International Association of Athletics Federations (IAAF), and World Anti-Doping Agency (WADA). Comprehensive reviews of relevant publications in social sciences, medical research, and law literature are presented. Additionally, analyses of mainstream media treatment of controversial topics, most notably doping, demonstrate how public opinion is influenced by such accounts, including those that perpetuate racist and sexist biases.

The lengthy list of online references indicates one of the benefits of the internet for researchers. Most were accessed in the period February 1, 2017 to February 9, 2018. Since July 2016, the topics of state-sponsored doping in Russia, suspensions of Russian athletes, and their subsequent appeals to CAS have dominated global attention, and will no doubt continue to generate a significant body of research and commentary in sports law and sports studies. Hunter and Shannon (2017) present a comprehensive review of these developments up to March 2017. Chapters 3 and 4 include discussion of the Russian controversies, including decisions rendered by CAS up to February 9, 2018.

Although many aspects of the CAS website, including earlier versions of the CAS Code, *TAS/CAS Bulletins*, and media releases are informative and comprehensive, its search engine is not always user-friendly. It is possible to identify some general trends by examining the details of decisions published at jurisprudence.tas-cas.org, but these online sources are incomplete because parties have the option of requesting confidentiality. An approximate estimate of the number of confidential decisions can be made by comparing the published decisions to the totals provided on the website under the heading Statistiques/Statistics (TAS-CAS, 2016b), and a recent detailed examination found that published CAS awards have, for decades, averaged below 30% of the total (Spera, 2017). As well as confirming the popular sentiment of keeping sport disputes 'within the family,' the large percentage of unpublished awards prevents any accurate quantitative analysis. In light of this deficit, I have prefaced my observations about trends by noting that I am commenting on published decisions only. In some instances, it appears that sports lawyers and legal scholars have had access to unpublished awards, and, where relevant, I have referred to unpublished cases mentioned in secondary sources. Similarly, some SFT decisions are published only in German, and again I relied on commentaries rather than original documents. In selecting specific CAS and SFT awards to examine in greater detail, I have been guided in part by experienced legal commentators who have identified these cases as significant.

Appeals involving men's professional football account for close to half of published CAS decisions, and, although there are important issues related to male players' nationalities and ethnicities, my current focus on gender required that I establish some limits to the scope of this research. For this reason, I have excluded most football cases, although some key decisions involving FIFA are included. Similarly, I have not examined the controversial 2016 Essendon case, which involved doping charges against 34 Australian Football League (AFL) players. The AFL tribunal had found the players not guilty, but WADA appealed their decision to CAS, which then imposed two-year suspensions. A number of issues in this case, including intent, due diligence, circumstantial evidence, jurisdiction, and the AFL's compulsory contractual powers have been examined in detail by other commentators (see, for example, Adair, 2016; Kanagaratnam, 2016).

The following discussion encompasses a period of approximately 35 years of Olympic industry and CAS history, with the endpoint for my research being February 9, 2018, the first day of the 2018 PyeongChang Winter Olympics. For the most part, the book is organized thematically rather than chronologically in order to focus on specific issues and controversies. In Part I, analyses of general trends in alternative dispute resolution (ADR) and debates over arbitration versus litigation serve to situate CAS in the broader international context. This section critiques historical and contemporary developments in sports law, the influence of sport exceptionalism as a guiding principle, the chronic problems of 'stacked decks' and 'repeat parties' in CAS disputes, and the impacts of gender in all these areas. Numerous examples of cases heard by CAS and the Swiss Federal Tribunal are analyzed in these chapters. Part II focuses on 'the war against doping' and the strict liability principle, as well as investigating the impacts of gender and 'race'/ethnicity on the outcomes of doping-related appeals. Issues of gender policing and gender variance are examined, with detailed critiques of medical research and media commentary concerning hyperandrogenism and the so-called 'testosterone advantage.' CAS decisions on matters of doping and discipline are examined. Throughout these discussions, I analyze how 'role model' rhetoric and 'level playing field' rationales are employed to justify draconian punishments imposed on athletes, whose basic human rights are often violated in the name of 'clean sport.'

PART I

CHAPTER 1

SPORTS LAW AND THE COURT OF ARBITRATION FOR SPORT

The IOC established the Court of Arbitration for Sport (CAS) in 1983 because of the perceived need within Olympic and international sport circles for a speedy, sport-specific and confidential dispute resolution process. The IOC, international federations (IFs), national Olympic committees (NOCs) and national sports organizations (NSOs) – that is, the most important Olympic industry players – were concerned about the 'intrusion of law into sport' and sought 'immunity from domestic jurisdictions' (Anderson, 2000, p. 123). Mainstream courts, proponents argued, were costly and time-consuming, and judges lacked specialized knowledge of sport-related matters. More ominously, according to veteran CAS arbitrator Richard McLaren, 'politics and economic incentives cast a darkening shadow across the playing field' (McLaren, 2001c, p. 379). In the oft-quoted words of another longstanding CAS arbitrator, Michael Beloff, 'Render unto sports the things that are sports and to courts the things that are legal' (Beloff, 2012, p. 80) – an overly simplistic formula and, arguably, a false dichotomy.

1.1. SPORTS, LAW, POLITICS

The notion that 'politics and sport don't mix,' or shouldn't mix, is a hoary chestnut that has been convincingly debunked by generations of progressive sport scholars dating back to the 1970s (see, for example, Bairner & Molnar, 2010; Brohm, 1978; Espy, 1979; Lenskyj & Wagg, 2012). On a global scale, the IOC's exercise of political power is exemplified through its 30-year relationship with the UN, and, as one critic noted, the IOC has moved from merely partnering with UN organizations to becoming 'a political insider at the UN' (van Luikj, 2017). One in seven NOCs around the globe has direct ties with that country's government (Play the Game, 2017). Sports and politics are certainly not strangers, as the following chapters will demonstrate.

In a 2012 commentary, Beloff observed that there were precedents to demonstrate 'the sensitivity of ordinary law to the peculiarities of sport,' giving as one example the UK's Sex Discrimination Act 1975, S.44, which exempted competitive sport from its protections (Beloff, 2012, p. 73). However, like S.19.2 of the 1981 Ontario Human Rights Code, discussed above, this so-called 'sensitivity' reflected binary thinking about gender and the uncritical embrace of sport exceptionalism — that is, the belief that sport is unique and requires its own special laws and rules, and that individuals outside of sport simply 'don't get it.' In a 2017 example, IOC president Thomas Bach accused critics of ignorance and selfishness. They were 'aggressive,' he claimed, and unwilling to engage in dialogue because they saw the IOC as part of the 'establishment' (Bach, quoted in Butler, 2017). In fact, the IOC's close relationship with national governments and multinational corporate sponsors provides ample evidence of its secure position within the 'establishment.'

Explaining some other features of sports law, Beloff pointed out that 'words which bear one meaning in ordinary legal instruments may bear another in instruments governing sport,' giving as examples cases where 'sporting nationality' differed from 'legal nationality' (Beloff, 2012, p. 74). In much the same way, the IOC has long had the power to confer or to refuse to confer 'country' status on contested territories. Similarly, the term 'independent' often takes on different meanings in sports law contexts. Although he was a CAS arbitrator, McLaren was identified as 'the Independent Person' in the report submitted to the World Anti-Doping Agency (WADA) in 2016, following his investigations into Russia's state-sponsored doping program. Similarly, in 2017, CAS arbitrator Beloff was appointed chair of the International Association of Athletics Federations (IAAF) Independent Disciplinary Tribunal. Regardless of these men's personal integrity, to the outside observer they do not appear *independent* in the usual sense of the word.

As I argued in a 2017 critique of 'Olympic ideals,' redefining words to fit the Olympic image is a convenient way to obscure its flaws (Lenskyj, 2017). In one example, anthropologist Susan Brownell made the confusing assertion that the 'Olympic movement' represents an 'alternative' system of defending human dignity. The Olympic Charter's reference to 'universal fundamental ethical principles,' she claimed, does not necessarily include what she referred to as the UN's and human rights movements' definitions of human rights – a strange distinction in light of the IOC's observer status at the UN and its long involvement in 'Sport in Development' partnerships with UN organizations. Instead, according to Brownell, the IOC 'defends human dignity with sport, fair play, friendship, and so on' (Brownell, 2012, pp. 128, 130).

These are more than simply matters of definition or semantics. Despite the fact that human rights violations in

China were virtually untouched by that country's hosting of the 2008 Beijing Olympics, and have escalated since then (Amnesty International, 2016), apologists relying on 'alternative' definitions can invoke the 'human dignity' argument, claiming that the Beijing Olympics achieved the goal of bringing humanity together to celebrate sport. The same false claims could be made for other recent host cities – Sochi, Vancouver, Sydney, Salt Lake City, and Atlanta, for example – while ignoring clear evidence that the human rights of Indigenous people, ethnic minorities, homeless people and protesters were violated (Lenskyj, 2000, 2002, 2008, 2014). Furthermore, as the following discussion will demonstrate, the language around the decades-long campaign to make sports law *special* threatens athletes' fundamental rights, and, ultimately, the integrity of sport.

In line with the emphasis on sports law as special is the requirement that specialist arbitrators deal with sport-related disputes. A counterargument holds that generalists, unlike specialists, are less likely to be biased as a result of their prior knowledge, thereby providing a forum where both parties have the opportunity to educate the arbitrator. Challenging my critique of sport-specific dispute resolution at a recent presentation, a sports lawyer in the audience sounded incredulous, asserting that those involved in sport-related cases *must* understand sport. What does this mean? They should value sport as a 'social good'? Believe in its purported magic and mystique? Understand the rules of play? Recognize its economic contribution? Play a sport themselves? Enjoy watching televised sport?

None of these requirements appear to be central to the judgement of CAS arbitrators. They rarely intervene in 'field of play' disputes. They appoint experts to assist on issues such as doping and gender identity. They need only 'a good knowledge of sport in general,' according to the CAS Code, and some appear to have less than that. The required 'competence' in sports law *and/or* international arbitration, as identified in the Code since 2004, means that some may have no actual sports law competence (TAS-CAS, 2016a). On the more nebulous 'social good' arguments, CAS decisions rarely invoke social or moral arguments, except in doping cases where they refer to the deterrent effects of sanctions and CAS's role in 'the fight against doping.' About one-quarter of CAS's published cases involve contract or transfer matters, mostly in football, and, like commercial contract disputes outside of sport, arbitrators examine similar basic issues: salary, breach of contract, compensation for damages, termination of contract, and other typical employment issues. Specialization in sports law is not necessarily a requirement for dealing with these kinds of disputes.

McLaren (1998) claimed that athletes' rights were central to the establishment of CAS, in part as a consequence of the IOC's 1986 suspension of the amateur rule and the growing numbers of professionals who participated in Olympic sport. Athletes increasingly recognized the economic implications of the sport—business—entertainment nexus and were demanding their rights. Insofar as 'rights' pertain to an individual athlete's career and livelihood, McLaren was correct in stating that the financial stakes had increased, but he may not have anticipated the recent rise in activism for *collective* rights, evident in the ongoing anti-racist protests initiated by African Americans and their supporters in the National Football League, or the growing strength of the World Players' Association (WPA). In fact, had CAS succeeded in protecting athletes' rights, including the right to full protection of the law and the presumption of innocence, WPA's 2017 Universal Declaration of Player Rights may have been unnecessary (World Players, 2017).

1.2. ALTERNATIVE DISPUTE RESOLUTION

The operation of CAS falls under the general heading of Alternative Dispute Resolution (ADR), a method of settling disputes, mostly commercial in nature, through mediation and/or arbitration. (Arbitration, and not mediation, will be the focus of this discussion.) ADR was developed in the 1970s as a cheaper and more flexible method than traditional litigation, which was criticized for its lengthy and costly adversarial proceedings. However, ADR's widespread popularity concealed numerous shortcomings, and by the 1990s, legal scholars and others were questioning whether the goals of fairness and justice were being met.

Whereas 1960s law reforms in western countries were shaped by the concepts of rights and justice, ADR rhetoric focused on harmony and efficiency, or as anthropologist Laura Nader termed it, harmony ideology, that is, 'the belief that harmony, in the guise of compromise or agreement is ipso facto better than an adversarial posture' (Nader, 1993, p. 3). Writing in 1993 about the American legal context, Nader presented an incisive critique of ADR as 'a coercive mechanism of pacification.' She explained how the alleged problems of 'too much litigation' and too much reliance on courts and the adversarial system had led to the widespread popularity of ADR, which was touted as protecting courts from overload, and freed them from so-called 'rubbish cases' concerning gender, the environment, and consumer issues.

1.2.1. ADR: A Feminist Alternative?

Not coincidentally, harmony ideology was compatible with feminist theories of the 1970s that emphasized the ethic of care and the special significance of connection and relationships in women's lives. According to this way of thinking, women spoke and reasoned *In a Different Voice*, as the title of Carol Gilligan's 1982 pioneering book suggested. In domestic disputes and divorce proceedings, for example, private mediation was seen as preferable to the public arena of family court, on the grounds that it produced inclusive solutions and preserved the family connections that women valued. While Gilligan based her theories on careful analysis of research findings, feminist scholars who followed her line of reasoning were often accused of biological determinism — in a few cases, a valid charge.

One of ADR's earliest American proponents, Carrie Menkel-Meadow, initially embraced Gilligan's arguments, most notably in a 1985 article titled 'Portia in a different voice: speculations on a women's lawyering process,' where she suggested that women's growing numbers in the legal profession would bring about more caring methods of dispute resolution (Menkel-Meadow, 1985). More recently, however, Menkel-Meadow has rethought her earlier position on the significance of gender. In a 2012 publication, she noted that research does not consistently demonstrate gender differences in ADR practice, and concluded that gender matters, but to different degrees and in different circumstances. Giving the specific example of cases involving a dangerous birth control device, the Dalkon Shield, she identified some 'gender-salient' issues where, she argued, gender does matter. Finally, she restated her position that diversity among dispute resolvers in terms of gender, ethnicity and social class 'is essential for democratic representation' and for extending the possibility of diverse ideas and approaches to problem-solving (Menkel-Meadow, 2012, p. 8).

On the broader issue of dispute resolution, Menkel-Meadow was critical of the cooptation of ADR and the 'privatization of justice,' in contrast to its initial goal of challenging 'formalistic and legalistic approaches to legal and social problem-solving' (Menkel-Meadow, 2013, p. 419). Moreover, the recent pattern where consumers and employees are contractually bound to mandatory arbitration results in private, unregulated and unreported outcomes that are not necessarily fair or just. The purported 'success' of ADR, notably the low rate of 2% of civil cases that proceed to full trial in the US, has had the unintended consequence of producing what critics consider 'an inadequate number for a democratic society to produce legal precedents and fair process.' Concerned about this cooptation, critics like Menkel-Meadow prefer the term 'appropriate dispute resolution' to demonstrate the need to recognize that 'one size of legal process does not fit all' (Menkel-Meadow, 2013, pp. 446, 423). This is a useful distinction in the context of sport-related disputes, many of which may be better suited to litigation than to arbitration.

Like virtually every other aspect of sport administration, CAS does not begin to meet the gender diversity criterion. Even when one takes into account the fact that opportunities for women to study law and/or to specialize in sports law are limited by cultural norms in many countries, there is a clear gender imbalance among CAS arbitrators. In 2016, 23 years after its creation, the International Council of Arbitration for Sport (ICAS), which provides oversight of CAS, finally achieved gender equality. Since 1996, the Ad Hoc Division (AHD) of CAS has heard appeals in Olympic host cities, but it was not until 2016 that the 12-member AHD at the Rio Olympics comprised equal numbers of women and men.

In the years since Menkel-Meadow's critique, there has been a groundswell of resistance to forced arbitration in the US, including a now-doomed move by two Democrat senators in 2016 to enact anti-forced arbitration laws, and the high-profile sexual harassment lawsuit filed in July 2016 by

Fox News journalist Gretchen Carlson against Fox CEO
Roger Ailes. Ailes's lawyers tried unsuccessfully to force the
case into arbitration based on a clause in Carlson's contract.
The case, which resulted in a confidential settlement of
US$20m and Ailes's swift departure from Fox, drew wide-
spread public attention to the pitfalls of arbitration (Diaz &
Dockterman, 2016).

1.3. INTERNATIONAL DISPUTES: (FORCED) ARBITRATION OR LITIGATION?

An overview of developments in international arbitration will
provide further context for a critical analysis of CAS's history
and functions. In commercial law circles, arbitration of international disputes has come to be viewed as the preferred
method of resolution, most notably because it avoids some of
the inherent problems of litigation, such as lengthy and
expensive court proceedings. Discussing international arbitration, Moses (2008) identified the following benefits: cases are
arbitrated in a neutral third country, parties may be represented by their regular counsels, and awards are more easily
enforced throughout the world through the New York
Convention on the Recognition and Enforcement of Foreign
Arbitral Awards, in force since 1958 and applicable to 157
contracting nation-states.

A detailed evaluation of the advantages and disadvantages
of arbitration was developed by Australian federal court
judge and independent arbitrator Kevin Lindgren. On the
positive side, he listed privacy, confidentiality and procedural
flexibility, facilitating lower costs and quicker outcomes.
Arbitration hearings are rarely open to the media or the public, with attendance usually limited to the parties themselves,
their legal representatives and transcribers. Personally or

commercially sensitive information can therefore be discussed in private. On the the issue of costs, however, he identified some disadvantages: if the case were litigated, expenses such as hearing room rental, transcription services and the judge's fee would be borne by taxpayers, rather than by the parties involved (Lindgren, 2016). CAS proceedings in Lausanne incur these kinds of costs, but hearings before AHD panels are free; in both instances, parties must pay for representation.

There are important distinctions between voluntary and forced arbitration, and the compliance demanded of athletes through their contracts with IFs and Olympic entry forms makes this an example of forced arbitration. As Comsti explained in a 2014 critique of forced arbitration in the US, there are 'fundamental differences' in 'knowledge, consent, and equal bargaining power between the individual employee and employer' (Comsti, 2014, p. 8). Forced arbitration, she argued, has developed into 'a juggernaut that has changed the nature of statutory enforcement of worker protection laws' and is 'an inadequate substitute for the public vindication of statutory workplace rights in our civil justice system' (Comsti, 2014, pp. 6, 9).

Commenting on general trends relating to involuntary arbitration and 'relationships of grossly disparate bargaining power,' American judges Craig Smith and Eric Moye concluded that 'law, including the FAA [Federal Arbitration Act] should be a shield for the weak and powerless and not a hammer for the strong and powerful' – a particularly apposite statement in relation to athletes' rights (cited in Comsti, 2014, p. 27). Although it serves IOC and CAS interests to promote sport exceptionalism and Olympic mystique – athletes as 'peace ambassadors' and members of one big 'Olympic family'– athletes are, in fact, workers, and the sporting arena is their workplace (e.g., McArdle, 2015, chapter 10; Sack & Staurowsky, 1998). As a consequence, it is reasonable to argue that they should enjoy the rights of similarly situated workers in their home countries.

As one critic asked, although athletes' contracts with NSOs were 'typical of private dispute resolution regulated in the code of civil procedure' (Wolf, 2014, p. 299), were their agreements really voluntary in a context where NSOs had the monopoly over their sport? However, Wolf concluded, somewhat optimistically, that NSOs' actions were scrutinized by human rights institutions, thus providing a 'link back to common good and the rule of law' (Wolf, 2014, p. 301). There is little evidence to support his optimism, although, as legal scholar Andrew Byrnes (2016, p.103) demonstrated, on the specific issue of anti-doping, external criticism and scrutiny as well as the efforts of 'internal human rights norm entrepreneurs working within CAS' have resulted in some improvements to the WADA Code. Overall, however, Byrnes concluded that such changes tended to focus on procedural rights, while substantive human rights violations continued to occur.

Comsti's points regarding the FAA's shortcomings are particularly relevant to CAS:

1. Forced arbitration is an inadequate substitute for the public vindication of statutory workplace rights in our civil justice system.

2. [It] stacks the decks in favor of employers.

3. Statistics show that workers lose more often, win smaller awards, and spend more money to prosecute their claims in forced arbitration than in court.

4. Forced arbitration shields employers from public accountability and judicial review when they violate the law. (Comsti, 2014, pp. 9, 10).

1.4. IOC AND CAS: GOVERNANCE ISSUES

Despite the IOC's status as a 'legal person' under Swiss law, it has more in common with the Church than with a business corporation, as sports law scholar Saul Fridman argued in a 1999 article. The Olympic Charter fails to include any provisions concerning members' and non-members' rights, managers' responsibilities, reporting and auditing requirements, remedies available to stakeholders, and so on, that are typically required under national incorporation legislation. Furthermore, like the Church, the IOC does not have democratically elected members, nor is it subject to national authorities or accountable to stakeholders. Finally, both the 'Olympic movement' and the Church are based on values established by a small group of individuals, and both purport to be self-regulating (Fridman, 1999, pp. 797–798). The IOC's subculture of bribery and corruption and the Church's record of inaction on child sexual abuse amply demonstrate these organizations' unwillingness and/or inability to regulate and discipline their own members, as well as their practice of actively protecting guilty parties from scrutiny or prosecution (Lenskyj, 2010).

Critics have shown how the IOC and IFs, unlike UN member states, are not bound by international treaties, laws or judicial bodies, rendering them 'a law unto themselves' (Munro, 2016, p. 7), or even 'a virtual world government' (Peacock, 2010). Whereas the 30 + UN organizations in 17 countries operate under standardized host country agreements, IFs are only subject to their own internal statutes, to CAS, and to the national laws and courts of the host country. Nor does IOC's observer status at the UN appear to carry any obligations regarding international laws and treaties. The majority of IFs are located in Switzerland and subject to its liberal laws, most notably the Swiss Private International Law Act.

Switzerland is undoubtedly a welcoming place for the world of sport. Amongst other benefits, it offers political neutrality, convenient geographical location and a low level of state regulation. Lausanne has been termed the 'Silicon Valley of sports,' with its recently constructed Maison du Sport International, a joint venture of the IOC, the canton of Vaud, and Lausanne, housing dozens of sports governing bodies (SGBs) for a total of more than 65 organizations within Switzerland (Ruiz, 2016a). However, international sports organizations found some of their freedoms curbed in 2015, when a new anti-corruption law included heads of sports organizations in the category of 'politically exposed persons,' thereby making it an automatic criminal offence for sport officials to be involved in bribery or other illegal activity. FIFA was the main target of this law, following the 2015 disclosure of corruption by FIFA officials. Before this change, Swiss courts required actual complaints to be lodged, before prosecuting private-sector offenders (Lee, 2017).

A 2013 Sport Governance Observer (SGO) survey investigated accountability and stakeholder representation in 35 SGBs, 27 of which were based in Switzerland. It examined a number of key indicators, including democratic elections, distribution of funding to member organizations, codes of ethics, ethics committees, mechanisms to prevent concentration of power, athletes' participation, regional representation, gender equality, and term limitations. The advocacy organization Right to Play, at the Danish Institute for Sport Studies in Copenhagen, was responsible for the SGO research. The study found the most glaring accountability deficits in distribution of funding and in the lack of independent ethics committees. Another major deficit related to gender: about 90% of the sports bodies had male presidents and male secretary generals; only 20 of the 35 had a female representative on their executive boards, and only 12 had more than one woman (Geeraet, Alm, & Groll, 2013, p. 208).

The issue of gender in sport governance was addressed during the November 2017 International Sports Law Journal (ISLJ) conference in The Hague in a discussion between sports lawyer Sean Cottrell and CAS arbitrator Michael Beloff. On the problem of women's underrepresentation, Beloff referred to recent sexual harassment controversies in UK sport, but said, as an aside, that he was not suggesting that every male administrator was 'a sporty equivalent of Harvey Weinstein,' a comment that amused some members of the audience (ISLJ, 2017). In fact, the same year, whistle-blowers had exposed the longstanding problem of a 'toxic culture' of bullying and harassment within SGBs, including the UK para-swimming and bobsleigh organizations and the Australian Olympic Committee (AOC culture, 2017; Ingle, 2017; Kelner, 2017). There is little reason to assume that male sport leaders will emerge unscathed from the global #MeToo campaign, as women continue to break the silence about sexual harassment in the workplace.

The IOC itself has long been criticized for its gender disparity; currently, only about 22% of its members are women. It was not until 1996, more than 30 years after the second wave of women's liberation movements in western countries, that the Olympic Charter was revised to include a specific reference to the promotion of women at all levels in sport, particularly in leadership, with the addition of Fundamental Principle 2. The first IOC World Conference on Women and Sport, held the same year, called for IFs and NOCs to create committees to promote this goal, with the modest requirement that by 2000, at least 10% of the members of the IOC, IFs and NOCs should be women (IOC, 1996, S. 2).

This is not to suggest that all advocates have to be female or that all women necessarily support efforts to achieve gender equality. However, given the glacial speed that has characterized social change in sport since the early 1900s, it is reasonable to assume that a critical mass of women in sport leadership, supported by male allies, is essential for any significant change to occur. Some critics go further, pointing to research showing that leadership diversity and gender equity constitute 'a risk management tool that could positively impact on integrity outcomes in sport' (Ordway & Opie, 2017, p. 48). Furthermore, as Nehme and Ordway (2016) argued, gender equity was a key priority for UNESCO, and WADA had collaborated with UNESCO on the 2005 UNESCO Anti-Doping Convention, therefore WADA should remedy its underrepresentation of women in its Foundation Board, at that time only 21%, and its Executive Committee, 25% (Nehme and Ordway, 2016, 229).

The 2013 SGO report also identified the problem of athletes' and other stakeholders' lack of decision-making power, and the 'monopolization of power,' evident in the dominance of European males who stayed in office for an average of 14 years (Geeraert et al., 2013, p. 212). In short, there was a pattern of abuse of sports organizations' autonomy, including the overall absence of 'proper procedures and tools against corruption, undemocratic procedures and other critical poor governance traits' (Munro, 2016, p. 7).

One observation that the report made concerning methodology is particularly telling. The researchers explained that they relied on the publicly available (online) statutes, constitutions and bylaws of the selected SGBs. No SGB heads responded to emailed requests for more detailed information – not an auspicious beginning to a study of organizations that have ostensibly been working on accountability and transparency (Geeraert et al., 2013, p. 194). It is possible, of course, that the reputation of Right to Play as a critical, action-based research and advocacy organization may have been a factor in their failure to respond.

1.5. CAS JURISDICTION: WHY? HOW?

In a 1983 *Olympic Review* article, Judge Keba M'Baye, IOC member from Senegal and CAS's founding president, stated that the CAS Code reflected emerging conventions and laws regarding arbitration, particularly the New York Convention (M'Baye, 1983, p. 763). However, rather than relying on the NY Convention's concept of nation-state, the IOC defines a member country according to its own rules. By giving recognition to a country's Olympic committee, the IOC grants it membership status and de facto political recognition (Espy, 1979, p. 29).

On the issue of CAS's jurisdiction, Rule 61 of the Olympic Charter states that any Olympic Games-related dispute 'shall be submitted *exclusively* to the CAS in accordance with the Code of Sports-Related Arbitration' (IOC, 2015a, emphasis added). Furthermore, in relation to CAS arbitration outside of Switzerland, Rule 61 grants CAS jurisdiction over athletes, NOCs, and international sport federations. The Olympic entry form must include all details of the Charter relevant to athletes, including, as Rule 44 states, the athlete's obligation 'to submit disputes to CAS jurisdiction.' On the question of disputes unrelated to the Olympics, CAS's jurisdiction is established through the rules and contracts of national and international sports governing bodies, specifically their arbitration clauses. CAS panels conduct *de novo* procedures, having 'full power to review the facts and the law… and issue a new decision' (TAS-CAS, 2017c, R57).

According to the CAS Code, the Swiss Federal Tribunal (SFT) is the only court that can exercise any influence over

CAS, although there have been a few notable exceptions in other European courts (discussed below). The limited grounds for SFT's overturning of a CAS award under Swiss Private International Law Act are as follows:

> *(i) the arbitral tribunal was not properly constituted, (ii) the arbitral tribunal wrongly accepted or declined jurisdiction, (iii) the arbitral tribunal ruled beyond the claims submitted to it, or failed to decide one or more of the claims submitted to it, (iv) the parties' fundamental procedural rights were breached, or (v) the award is incompatible with public policy. (Rigozzi, 2010, p. 219)*

Whether athletes, either voluntarily or not, can waive the right to a court hearing is a key question. In a 1998 commentary, McLaren portrayed CAS as a benefit for athletes: 'Athletes did not give up their legal rights within their national and international governing bodies or their national courts, but had an immediate and additional adjudicative body to which reference of sports-specific disputes could be made during the Games' (McLaren, 1998, p. 4). Although his statement appears to contradict the restriction stated in Rule 61 (which first appeared in the 1995 version of the Olympic Charter as Rule 74), there have been some challenges in national courts.

On the question of forced arbitration, a landmark 2007 decision of SFT involving doping allegations against professional tennis player Guillermo Canas established that athletes were not exercising 'free will' when they signed contracts with NSOs. Noting that, unlike the parties in international commercial contracts, athletes were not on an equal footing with SGBs, the decision stated:

> *[...] experience has shown that, by and large, athletes will often not have the bargaining power*

> *required and would therefore have to submit to the*
> *federation's requirements, whether they like it or*
> *not. Accordingly, any athlete wishing to participate*
> *in organised competition under the control of a*
> *sports federation whose rules provide for recourse to*
> *arbitration will not have any choice but to accept*
> *the arbitral clause [...]. (cited in Rigozzi, 2010,*
> *pp. 227–228)*

SFT annulled CAS's 2005 decision on procedural grounds, that is, Canas's right to be heard, noting that the waiver regarding appeals to SFT in the Association of Tennis Professionals' contract was not enforceable. The revised CAS award (CAS, 2007/A/951) partially upheld his appeal, reducing the period of ineligibility, but, as sports lawyer Antonio Rigozzi emphasized, 'the decision shall not be interpreted as questioning (or be used to question) the validity of the arbitration agreements contained in sports regulations' (Rigozzi, 2010, p. 228). This did not mean, however, that the validity of such clauses would not be challenged in the future.

Former IOC president Samaranch is credited with proposing the establishment of CAS. 'His Excellency,' as he preferred to be called, envisioned 'a kind of court for the sports world,' later characterized as 'a supreme court for world sport' (McLaren, 2010, 306). In fact, it should not be called a court at all. As the French title Tribunal Arbitral du Sport accurately reflects, it is an arbitration tribunal. In view of the bribery and corruption scandals that flourished on Samaranch's watch, one might question his motives for seeking this kind of 'immunity,' which would preserve the IOC's power and, when necessary, remove disputes from global media scrutiny.

In the first 10 years of CAS's operation, the IOC's control, symbolized by Samaranch's presidency of both organizations, was largely unchallenged, and the small number of disputes brought to CAS by athletes and/or sports organizations between 1983 and 1993 suggested that they questioned its impartiality. It was not until 2003 that the annual number of CAS cases finally reached 100, and, in 2004, there was a related spike in the number of appeals to SFT (Duval & Marino, 2014). There is little evidence that sport-related disputes were causing an undue burden on domestic courts or that parties were frustrated by slow decisions or judges' lack of sport expertise. Regardless, the vast majority of justifications for CAS pointed to the pressing need for athletes and SGBs to have sport-specific dispute resolution procedures that were faster, more flexible and less costly than litigation. Certainly the AHD panels at Olympic Games came closest to achieving those goals, but they were not a feature of CAS until 13 years after it was established, and so were not a key part of the founders' rationales.

The benefits of CAS, as expressed by sports lawyers, arbitrators, and others included:

- 'expedient, flexible, inexpensive and informed judgments' outside of the court system (Kane, 2003, p. 2);

- 'neutrality, efficiency and the input of experts' (Anderson, 2000, p. 126);

- 'fair and even-handed' (McLaren, 2001a, p. 516); and

- effective dispute resolution 'within the Family of Sport' (Blackshaw, 2003, p. 61).

The popular 'potted history' approach to CAS routinely begins by crediting Samaranch for its origins, and acknowledging its less than stellar performance during the first 10 years. These accounts then point to the reform of 1994, and describe CAS's history since that time in generally glowing

terms. Emphasizing the extent of this 'before and after' trans-
formation, some commentators repeated critiques expressed
in the first decade, including allegations that CAS was merely
'a court of vassals of the IOC brought along to the Games to
do its bidding' (McLaren, 2001c, 382), 'small siblings of the
IOC,' and 'minions for the "Lord of the Rings"' (Anderson,
2000, p. 125).

For CAS to be effective, the IOC needed to persuade all
IFs to agree to use it rather than their own internal dispute
resolution bodies. Among the first to do so was the
Fédération Equestre Internationale, respondent in German
equestrian Elmar Gundel's unsuccessful appeals to CAS and
subsequently to SFT, discussed below. The FIFA and the
IAAF were slow to sign on, despite their expressed interest in
a harmonized approach to doping at a 1993 meeting of the
IOC Executive. Also present at that meeting were seven
representatives from the Association of Summer Olympic
Games International Federations, one of whom, Joao
Havelange, was head of FIFA. Twenty IFs agreed to a unified
anti-doping approach, and, in the same 'common spirit,' they
supported the creation of a 'supreme' arbitration body, later
known as the ICAS, to oversee CAS (Major breakthrough,
1993, p. 299).

1.6. A NEW LEAF? 1994 CAS REFORMS

The reforms introduced in 1994 were prompted by the 1993
SFT decision in the Gundel case. After the CAS panel ruled
that Gundel's horse had been doped (TAS 92/63), he
appealed to SFT on the grounds that CAS failed to meet the
independence and impartiality requirements of 'a true arbitral
tribunal.' Although SFT judges rejected his appeal, they noted
in an *obiter dictum* (incidental remarks) that there were

problems with CAS's 'organic and economic ties with the IOC' regarding costs and appointment of members. Particularly if the IOC were a party in a dispute, SFT noted, CAS's independence would be in question (Kane, 2003, pp. 5, 6). Significantly, SFT has rejected a number of similar challenges regarding CAS's lack of independence in the period since 1993, as has a state court in Australia (McLaren, 2010, p. 308).

Without external pressure, it appears that the IOC's direct control over CAS may have lasted indefinitely. Keeping up appearances, Samaranch implied that, in its wisdom and benevolence, the IOC itself had initiated the reforms. 'In order to protect the athlete, we have created the Court of Arbitration for Sport, and over it, the International Council of Arbitration for Sport, which is independent of the IOC […],' he announced at the 102nd IOC Session in 1994, the year that the UN had declared the 'International Year of Sport and the Olympic Ideal' (Samaranch, 1994, p. 64). CAS Secretary General Gilbert Schwaar also noted, with some indignation, that an appellant (Gundel) had attempted 'to contest the very existence of the CAS,' and that SFT had confirmed that CAS was 'a real arbitral court.' Neglecting to acknowledge the SFT's rather pointed *dictum* in the Gundel decision, Schwaar stated that, 'With the intent of safeguarding even better the rights of the parties […] it was decided […] to create [the ICAS] […] to make the CAS wholly independent of the IOC …' (Schwaar, 1993, p. 305).

Despite the reform efforts, significant ties continued to exist between the IOC and CAS, most notably the IOC's financial support, its powerful role in the appointment of CAS members, and its ability to change CAS statutes. The IOC purportedly handed over control of CAS to ICAS, a 20-person body that elects CAS members, and is also supported financially by the IOC. After the restructuring, CAS comprised a minimum of 150 panelists with a balance between sport and legal expertise – a move viewed as strengthening its independence and impartiality. According to most sources, CAS had now achieved independence from the IOC, with ICAS credited for serving as 'a layer of insulation' between the IOC and CAS (McLaren, 2001a, p. 519).

However, as McLaren also noted, the IOC retained control over the appointment of CAS's president long after ICAS was established, with its founding president, IOC member Judge Keba M'baye, heading both organizations from 1984 until his death in 2007 (McLaren, 2010, 310). The internal structure supported by the 2016 Code of Sports-related Arbitration (TAS-CAS, 2016a) continues in that tradition: the ICAS president is also the CAS president, and the IOC's influence has been maintained with the 2007 appointment of IOC vice-president John Coates, and his re-election in 2015, as president of ICAS. As specified in the Code, the IOC nominates the ICAS president, and selects four IOC representatives. IFs and the Association of National Olympic Committees each select four individuals, who can be members or non-members. The group of 12 then selects four more members 'with a view towards safeguarding the interests of the athletes,' and the group of 16 chooses the remaining four. Unlike the IOC itself, which has representatives from the IOC Athletes' Commission elected by athletes, CAS only permits athletes to have indirect input into the appointment of arbitrators. On that issue, a change in the 2016 Code invited the athletes' commissions associated with the IOC, IFs and NOCs to propose names to ICAS.

In its revised format, CAS introduced two arbitration divisions: the Ordinary Division, which deals with initial cases, and the Appeals Division, which reviews decisions made by SGBs. Each case is heard by a three-person panel, one chosen by each party and the third by those two arbitrators, or the appellant may choose a sole arbitrator. A regional office in Denver, later moved to New York, began operation in 1996 in order to extend CAS's range to North America, and an Oceania site was established in Sydney prior to the 2000 Olympics. AHDs, which operate during the Olympics and other international competitions, comprise two co-presidents and 12 arbitrators; a panel of three, or a sole arbitrator selected by the presidents, hears disputes within 24 hours. While this process guarantees speedy outcomes, appellants lack the option of choosing from a list of over 350 arbitrators, a choice they would have if their appeals were conducted at CAS. Despite the apparent legal anomaly of creating off-shore, 'pop-up' tribunals, the legitimacy of AHDs has rarely been questioned. With both IOC and CAS headquarters located in Lausanne, Switzerland, CAS arbitration is governed by Swiss law, even when hearings are held elsewhere, as is the case with AHD cases. This jurisdictional arrangement serves the interests of the Olympic industry well, by contributing to the immunity from domestic courts that the IOC and IFs were seeking.

1.7. REPEAT PARTIES – SGBS AND SPORTS LAWYERS

Corporations that are 'repeat parties' to arbitrations enjoy significant advantages, having greater knowledge of arbitrators' patterns and practices than most disputants (Lindgren, 2016). This imbalance is especially apparent in relation to CAS appeals. Unlike individual athletes, the IOC, WADA, and major IFs such as FIFA, Fédération Internationale de Natation (FINA) and IAAF have several decades of experience with familiar CAS arbitrators, and most use law firms that have long histories with CAS. Rigozzi was one of the few commentators to take a position on the problem of arbitrators who were repeatedly selected by SGBs, writing in 2010: 'If the nomination of an arbitrator by a party is quasi-systematic, I do not believe his independence to be objectively guaranteed; in particular, if such nominations occurred in very similar cases, for example in doping matters' (Rigozzi, 2010, p. 238).

The 'insider' advantages that SGBs enjoy stand in stark contrast to the barriers confronting an athlete like 19-year-old Indian sprinter Dutee Chand, who was eventually represented by counsel from Toronto, Canada, after interventions on her behalf were made by her supporters in India and internationally in 2015 (see Chapter 4). Obviously, parties benefit from having representatives with sports law knowledge as well as general arbitration competence, and their preference for experienced lawyers is reflected in the relatively small number of firms involved in CAS cases. Rigozzi, Besson, and McAuliffe (2016, p. 2) noted that, because appellants look for experienced counsel, and because, in his view, CAS is 'not a forum in which [...] lawyers can easily "cut their teeth",' there is a 'vicious cycle' that makes it difficult for new counsel to gain experience and recruit clients. Furthermore, given the high incidence of sports governing bodies, particular IFs, appearing as repeat parties in CAS disputes, the 'repeat' lawyers are likely to have more experience in representing powerful 'Olympic family' members than individual athletes. Unsurprisingly, the IOC and the major IFs – FIFA and IAAF, for example – tend to be represented by the same counsel and/or law firms year after year.

Just as Switzerland is over-represented in terms of CAS arbitrators, it is also home to specialized sports law firms whose counsel are repeat parties in a significant number of CAS cases. Added to these are a small number of firms outside of Europe that take on cases from Arab countries, Asia and South America, the latter being for the most part football-related. One popular firm, Kellerhals Carrard, has four offices in Switzerland and one in Shanghai. On its website, the Lausanne office points to its team's extensive experience with CAS and the IOC, most notably its senior partner, Francois Carrard, who was the IOC's Director General from 1989 to 2003. Carrard achieved a high media profile as IOC spokesman in his last few years of office, as the bribery and corruption scandals and subsequent inquiries were unfolding.

Carrard's name appeared as a CAS arbitrator in 14 published cases, one in 1986, and the rest in the period 1995–2008. If the record is accurate, this could suggest that, between 1995 and 2003, he was both an IOC employee and a CAS arbitrator (in five cases). In his more recent role as counsel in 21 CAS cases, he represented the IOC in 14. Other members of the Kellerhals Carrard team were equally active, and the firm had a relatively high success rate when representing IFs and WADA. If an individual athlete wanted – and could afford – the most experienced representation, Kellerhals Carrard would be the one to choose. However, advertising on the firm's website <kellerhals-carrard.ch/en > is directed more toward sports organizations than individuals: '[…] clients include multisport bodies (such as the IOC and WADA), International Federations, National Anti-Doping Agencies as well as a host of Football Federations and clubs.'

Several of the 'repeat' counsel in CAS disputes moved from representing clients at CAS to becoming CAS arbitrators, or, before changes to ICAS/CAS statutes that stopped this practice, combining both roles, thus potentially raising conflict of interest concerns. According to published cases on the TAS/CAS website, one person appears to have represented parties in seven CAS cases between 1998 and 2004, while at the same time serving on AHD panels at the 1996, 2000 and 2004 Olympics. Another CAS arbitrator participated in over 70 panels in the period 1998–2016, while, as counsel he represented six parties between 1992 and 2006. A third person, a CAS arbitrator since 2002, represented parties in two CAS cases, in 2006 and 2009.

Among the very active CAS arbitrators is Michele Bernasconi, a partner with the Zurich firm Bar and Karrer, who, according to published records, served on 128 panels in total, 83 of which were football-related. At a similar high level of participation is Luigi Fumagalli, with over 100 cases, 61 football related – about 10% of the total appeals involving football.

These patterns among arbitrators did not go unnoticed by the parties involved. In 2011, in two consolidated appeals of the Union Cyclisme Internationale (UCI) and WADA, against RFEC (the Spanish cycling federation) and a Spanish Tour de France cyclist, both WADA and UCI nominated Quentin Byrne-Sutton as arbitrator. Challenging the nomination, RFEC requested that Byrne-Sutton disclose the number of CAS cases where WADA or another anti-doping organization had nominated him as arbitrator (CAS, 2011/A/2384).

According to published figures on CAS database, from 2002 to 2011, Byrne-Sutton had been an arbitrator for about 10 doping-related cases. In three of these, WADA, represented by a Kellerhals-Carrard lawyer, was appellant; two appeals were upheld, and one partially upheld. In two other cases, WADA was respondent, and both were upheld. No further information on the nomination process was provided, but presumably the answer satisfied the respondents, who then nominated Ulrich Haas, and these two arbitrators selected Efraim Barak to preside over the panel. The panel partially upheld UCI's and WADA's appeals, but, as in other doping cases, changed the start date for the cyclist's ineligibility to credit the period served during his provisional suspension (CAS, 2011/A/2384).

By 2010, the Statutes of ICAS and CAS (the Code) were revised to include clause S18: 'CAS arbitrators and mediators may not act as counsel for a party before the CAS.' But, as Secretary General Mathieu Reeb confirmed in a *CAS Bulletin* article, if a CAS arbitrator were to act as counsel, 'his/her function [...] will not be called into question in the arbitration at stake' (Reeb, 2010, p. 32). Instead, ICAS was empowered to deal with the person as they chose, a loophole that some critics identified as weakening the attempt to prevent conflict of interest (Brubaker & Kulikowski, 2010). Furthermore, for ICAS to deal with a party's challenge of an arbitrator would add extra time to a process that purportedly relied on speed and efficiency. Reeb also 'emphasized' that the new rule did not restrict colleagues in the same law firm as the CAS arbitrator from representing parties in a dispute. However, as early as 2004, S11 of the Code had ruled against exactly that practice, and the 2017 version continues to do so (TAS-CAS, 2017c).

It could be argued that IOC members are not in conflict of interest when they serve as CAS arbitrators in cases not controlled by IFs directly connected to the IOC. It is difficult to find those few exceptions – the World Chess Federation, for example – and relatively easy to identify cases that raise conflict of interest concerns. Denis Oswald, IOC member since 1991, served as counsel in three CAS cases between 1986 and 2001, and has been a CAS arbitrator on 48 cases since 1998, several years after the reforms were introduced to render CAS more independent of the IOC. Parties in Oswald's cases included the IFs for gymnastics, swimming, equestrian, judo and hockey, all Olympic sports. In a 1993 Swiss case involving a dispute in ice hockey, a sport governed by an IF, two of the three CAS arbitrators, Oswald and Marc Hodler, were IOC members (CAS 93/103), and a 1994 appeal to CAS was heard by two IOC members, Agustin Arroyo and

Richard Pound (CAS 94/132). Five years later, Arroyo, IOC member from Ecuador, was expelled following investigations into bribery and corruption allegations conducted by the IOC's Ad Hoc Commission of Inquiry, which Pound chaired.

1.8. CONCLUSION

In the broader context of alternative dispute resolution, CAS is subject to many of the same shortcomings as non-sport tribunals, including repeat parties, stacked decks and forced arbitration. Appellants are disadvantaged when facing powerful organizations represented by highly experienced (and expensive) counsel. Despite the purported 'user-friendly' features of ADR and its early association with feminist thinking, it does not necessarily protect the interests of the less powerful party. CAS's close association with the IOC and the global Olympic industry creates the potential for even greater inequalities and injustices, with poor governance contributing to these problems. Most attempts at reform within CAS have not fully addressed the serious issues of lack of independence and conflict of interest on the part of arbitrators. The next chapter will continue to evaluate CAS in relation to critiques of general arbitration, as well as examining developments in the general campaign to promote sport autonomy – a code name for sport exceptionalism.

CHAPTER 2

CAS AND SPORT EXCEPTIONALISM

For 35 years, proponents of alternative dispute resolution through CAS, the 'supreme court for sport', have relied on speed, efficiency and privacy arguments, while consideration of athletes' rights and the pursuit of justice remain secondary. According to the sport exceptionalism argument, dispute resolution within the 'family of sport' is far preferable to public litigation. Reputations within the 'small world of sport' are 'worth preserving', lest disputes damage fan support and team morale, in other words, the bottom line (Morek, 2012).

2.1. ALTERNATIVE DISPUTE RESOLUTION AND CONFIDENTIALITY

Although privacy is routinely cited as a benefit of ADR, it is not necessarily in the athlete's or public interest to keep dispute proceedings private and confidential. The level of media scrutiny of all Olympic-related controversies is extremely high, and it could therefore be argued that first-hand, accurate accounts of hearings are preferable to hearsay. Moreover, privacy may be valued more by one party than by the other. Given the power differential between an individual athlete and a sports organization, complete transparency would probably benefit the athlete in the long run. Sports lawyer Mark Mangan points out, however, that, unlike the more common policy in commercial arbitration where the default position is confidentiality, the CAS Code only keeps awards confidential if one party requests it. On the issue of greater transparency, he recommended open proceedings which 'would discourage unmeritorious claims and appeals... and spread important messages about... the fight against doping.' Published decisions have generated a useful body of case law, known as *lex sportiva*, he claimed, but he also acknowledged that, while other arbitral panels frequently consult precedents, the CAS Code does not formally recognize the *stare decisis* (precedent) principle (Mangan, 2009, p. 598). In short, privacy is a mixed blessing for the parties involved, as well as for future appellants.

For their part, unsurprisingly, CAS's proponents frequently invoked the privacy issue and the importance of keeping disputes 'within the family of sport.' According to Blackshaw, perhaps unwittingly echoing Carol Gilligan, ADR 'facilitates the restoration and maintenance of personal and business relationships.' The benign-sounding 'family of sport' metaphor resembles 'Olympic family' rhetoric invoked by IOC and bid committee members who were embroiled in the bribery and corruption scandals of 1999–2000. Exchanges of expensive gifts and other 'benefits', according to these men, simply demonstrated the depth of ties among members of the 'Olympic family' (Lenskyj, 2000, chapter 3).

More importantly, and arguably a higher priority for SGBs, Blackshaw claimed that this strategy avoided the problem of sports bodies and sports people having to 'wash their dirty sports linen in public' (Blackshaw, 2003, p. 57). McLaren similarly claimed that athletes valued the confidentiality of arbitration proceedings in order to avoid being called cheats and ostracized by their peers (McLaren, 1998) — a view that seems a little dated 20 years later, given the almost daily exposés of doping and the mainstream media's fondness for applying the 'drug cheat' label. Furthermore, an argument can be made that it is in the public interest to promote open and transparent resolution of all sport-related disputes, given the significant amounts of public money that support high performance sport, especially the Olympic Games.

Regardless of the self-serving desire for privacy, the FIFA bribery scandals of 2008 resulted in a fairly substantial public airing of 'dirty sports linen.' Following a four-year investigation, a court in Zug, Switzerland, found Joao Havelange, FIFA president until 1998, together with Brazilian football head Ricardo Teixeira and other FIFA officials, guilty of having received illegal payments from ISL Sports Marketing. Their names were not revealed until 2010 when SFT lifted the Zug court's gag order, following challenges by media organizations (Former FIFA boss, 2012). Fifteen years earlier, expressing support for a harmonized approach to doping through WADA, ICAS and CAS, Havelange had agreed with his fellow IF leaders that 'we must settle our problems with our own jurisdictions' (quoted in Major breakthrough, 1993, p. 300). Sepp Blatter, Havelange's successor as FIFA president, was suspended in 2015 following charges of criminal mismanagement, and FIFA Ethics Committee banned him from any involvement in FIFA for eight years, later reduced to six; Blatter's appeal to CAS in 2016 was unsuccessful (CAS 2016/A/4501).

Interestingly, another IF president who, like Havelange, had supported the WADA initiative promoting harmonized doping policies in 1993 was Peter Tallberg, president of the

International Sailing Federation. Around the same time, Toronto was bidding for the 2000 Olympics under the leadership of former Olympic yachtsman Paul Henderson, and the benefits of 'Olympic family' ties that Tallberg enjoyed included a job for his son in Henderson's company. As the bribery scandals were exposed, Tallberg, whose sons had also been given employment in two other bid cities, told journalists, 'The IOC has no rules against normal and family connections' (quoted in Saunders & Partridge, 1999).

2.2. CONTRIBUTION TO THE DEVELOPMENT OF LAW

In precedential judicial systems, litigation through the courts serves an important public interest by establishing precedents, whereas arbitration does not. Despite this feature of general arbitration, CAS arbitration purports to be an exception, and its proponents note with approval the development of *lex sportiva*, a coined term that refers to global sports law (see, for example, Casini, 2011; Foster, 2003, 2005; McLaren, 1998, 2010; Mitten, 2014). On the question of precedent, Nafziger explained, 'A fully developed *lex sportiva* would help apply three values that the principle of *stare decisis* serves: efficiency of the legal process, predictability or stability of expectations: and equal treatment of similarly situated parties' (Nafziger, 2006, p. 50). It is difficult to find evidence that CAS decisions consistently meet these criteria.

In two critical commentaries, Foster (2003, 2005) identified contradictions in CAS's application of different legal concepts covered by the term *lex sportiva*. He differentiated between 'international sports law', as applied by national courts, and 'global sports law', which as he demonstrated was 'a cloak for continued self-regulation [by IFs] [...] and a claim for non-intervention by national legal systems and by international sports law' (2003, p. 35). CAS operated primarily as a 'standards council' and rarely overturned IF decisions (Foster, 2005, p. 2). In effect, IFs signed on to a private and 'sacrosanct' system of governance that demanded immunity from interventions by national and domestic legal systems. CAS considered itself to be 'the only system capable of international applicability and consistency for international sport' (Valloni, 2012). Foster concluded that self-regulation regarding the rules of the game and the ethical principles of sport was appropriate but argued that parties should have access to national courts where decisions related to 'the spirit of the game' caused economic damage. 'General principles of the rule of law', he argued, 'must be applied either by transnational arbitration or by national courts' (Foster, 2003, p. 16).

Examining how CAS functions in relation to precedent, critics have identified a number of contradictions. In a review of cases before 2002, Oschutz noted that CAS panels were 'not generally bound to follow earlier decisions or rules of *stare decisis*' but were 'disposed' to do so 'to strengthen legal predictability in international sport law' (Oschutz, 2002, p. 680). Straubel's more critical analysis identified inconsistencies in CAS's functioning, most notably, whether it worked as a private settlement body with informal, confidential proceedings, or a public settlement body that creates precedents and operates like a regular court (Straubel, 2005, p. 1211). In a comprehensive critique, McArdle wrote: '[...] a cynic might argue that CAS Panels use precedent when doing so reinforces the judgment they wish to reach and ignore it when the precedents are adverse [...]' (McArdle, 2015, p. 33). Having demonstrated how sports decision makers in the Oscar Pistorius case had demonstrated 'procedural ineptitude, mendacity or sheer incompetence', McArdle recommended that CAS pay more attention to precedent:

> *The application of a coherent corpus of arbitration*
> *principles to sport dispute resolution would be*
> *particularly welcome if it were to be underpinned by*
> *a greater willingness on the part of the CAS to make*
> *explicit reference to its own earlier determinations,*
> *as well as to wider legal authority. (McArdle, 2015,*
> *p. 34)*

The low percentage of published decisions also contributes to problems relating to precedent. As sports lawyer Sean Cottrell noted in a 2017 discussion with Michael Beloff, those counsel with years of experience representing repeat parties such as WADA, FIFA, FINA or IAAF have access to unpublished decisions, which they can introduce into the hearing to support their clients' cases. If counsel for the other party – usually an individual athlete or team – are unfamiliar with these unpublished decisions, they have limited time to read them. Furthermore, as Cottrell pointed out, parties from some countries lack 'legal IQ' and are disadvantaged in terms of choosing the most appropriate arbitrator. Inside knowledge of arbitrators who tended to take pro-athlete decisions was also an advantage not shared by all appellants. Conversely, Beloff acknowledged that he had 'regular clients', presumably those who nominated him based on positive past experiences, but noted that Blatter was the only party who had successfully objected to his selection, alleging lack of impartiality (ISJL, 2017).

2.3. THE COSTS ISSUE

As increasing numbers of appeals were brought to CAS, the costs to athletes became the subject of criticism, with some estimates of fees as high as CAN\$ 100,000 (Coletta, 2015). Costs include CAS application fee, administrative costs, fees for arbitrators and clerk (if applicable), 'a contribution towards the expenses of the CAS', and payments to witnesses, experts and interpreters (TAS-CAS, 2017c, R64.4). CAS proceedings involving appeals against decisions issued by IFs or other sport bodies that are disciplinary in nature are free, as are appeals to AHDs. Bar associations in recent Olympic host cities have provided pro bono counsel for athletes. For their part, commentators tended to view CAS costs as 'modest' compared to other arbitral bodies, in part because arbitrators usually accept a fee that is lower than their commercial hourly rate (Reilly, 2012, 73, Rigozzi et al., 2016, 5 fn. 16). Of course, for many athletes with limited experience in these matters, comparisons with other rates may be meaningless.

In 2012, a system of legal aid was introduced, but a closer look reveals some potential pro-CAS bias. For example, CAS selects and compiles a list of pro bono counsel, whose names are given to applicants, and ICAS evaluates all legal aid requests, giving only 'brief' reasons for its decisions. Although the procedure of granting legal aid is confidential, CAS 'must inform' the panel and the other parties that the applicant has received legal aid, a disclosure that reveals the financial straits of the athlete (TAS-CAS, 2013). An example of a more equitable legal aid system is that of Ontario, where the program is administered by an independent, non-profit corporation that is publicly funded and publicly accountable, with lawyers signing on, rather than being handpicked by the body that administers the program (Legal Aid Ontario, 2016).

On the issue of costs, SFT judges in a 2011 decision – one of the rare successful appeals – expressed concern about CAS arbitrators' 'discretion to grant the prevailing party a contribution towards its legal fees and other expenses' taking into account the 'complexity and outcome of the proceedings, as well as the conduct and financial resources of the parties' (TAS-CAS, 2017c, R64.5). The decision noted that this rule does not give parties 'the right to submit evidence as to costs', that is, the right to be heard (due process). It further stated that 'to guarantee some equal treatment, it would be desirable for the CAS to specify the concept of "contribution" [...] to give a framework' to arbitrators on this matter (SFT 4A_600/2010).

It is not difficult to see the potential problems with the wording of this rule in the Code. Can an individual athlete expect a more generous 'contribution' than a wealthy SGB? Does 'conduct' refer to the alleged misdemeanor, or to remorse, or to behavior during the hearing? While agreeing that a framework would increase predictability, Rigozzi et al. stated their belief that it was unnecessary as long as arbitrators acted ethically and justified their cost-related decisions (Rigozzi et al., 2016, p. 5, n. 14). The Swiss Arbitration Decisions commentary noted that it was unclear whether or not the suggestion was 'a mere *dictum*' (passing remark) but agreed that, on the issue of costs, international arbitrators in Switzerland would be 'well advised to systematically give the parties' the chance to provide evidence of their expenses (CAS award, 2011). Unlike the structural change that CAS had made after SFT's *dictum* in the Gundel case, CAS only added a clause to Rule 64.5: 'As a general rule, *and without any specific request from the parties*, the panel has the discretion to grant the prevailing party a contribution [...]' (TAS-CAS, 2017a, emphasis added).

In the usual contradictory rhetoric of Olympic industry officials, CAS secretary Matthieu Reeb identified CAS's new legal aid system as evidence of recent progress, but proceeded to reveal a different perspective on the matter of costs. In 2016, discussing Olympic athlete Claudia Pechstein's seven-year legal battle with the IOC through CAS and European courts (see Chapter 3), he claimed that similar challenges were unlikely because 'I don't think every athlete in the world can afford this kind of marathon' (quoted in Ruiz, 2016b). In other words, CAS has the upper hand as long as the IOC guarantees its financial support, albeit redirected through ICAS. On the question of CAS's independence from the IOC, the *New York Times* article on the Pechstein case pointed out that one of CAS's new arbitrators, Tricia Smith, was also a member of the IOC, thereby joining four others who belonged to both organizations (Ruiz, 2016b). Smith, together with IOC members Richard Pound and Denis Oswald, also served on the IOC's Legal Affairs department.

2.4. OLYMPIC CHARTER VS NATIONAL COURTS

In the broader context of world politics, the Olympic Charter, first formalized in 1978, is commonly viewed as customary international law, with the IOC, CAS and WADA exercising rational-legal authority on sport matters (Peacock, 2010, pp. 323, 324). One sports lawyer noted, without apparent irony, 'it is indeed amazing that a document issued by a private Swiss corporation has assumed all the features of an international treaty' (Mestre, 2007, p. 7). Amazing, indeed, but, on the issue of international influence, the IOC freely exercised its pseudo-governmental power when it served Olympic industry interests, for example, by granting political recognition to the NOCs of contested countries. On the other hand, when rationalizing its laissez-faire approach to other political issues, it invoked its non-governmental status by claiming, for example, that it was powerless to intervene on human rights violations in host countries.

As Mestre explained, the Charter is a 'heterogeneous legal text' that 'enshrines' the IOC's executive and judicial powers

and sets out technical rules and codes of conduct. He attrib-
uted its staying power to an 'extra-legal' feature – its alleged
'moral authority' (Mestre, 2007, p. 7). National courts have
frequently deferred to the IOC's authority and/or CAS's jurisdiction, for example in gender discrimination cases such as
the men-only 5000 m and 10000 m athletic events in the
1984 Los Angeles Olympics and the men-only ski-jump
events in the 2010 Vancouver Olympics, as well as legal disputes between the IOC and Gay Games organizers over the
use of the word *Olympics* in the 1980s. In these kinds of
cases, national courts have avoided clashes with the IOC and
international federations, bodies that are not bound by the
anti-discrimination laws of the host country. Moreover, there
is little evidence that any sports governing body takes seriously the Olympic Charter's Fundamental Principle 6, promoting the practice of sport 'without discrimination of any
kind', as amply illustrated in the ski-jump case.

In the lead-up to the Vancouver 2010 Winter Olympics, a
group of 15 female ski jumpers asked the Vancouver
Organizing Committee (VANOC) to include ski jump events
for women as well as for men. Following mediation at the
Canadian Human Rights Commission in 2008, the federal
government and sport minister announced their support for
the ski-jumpers' request, but later that year, a newly elected
sport minister claimed that the decision was up to the IOC.
He was, in fact, correct, and as some observers pointed out,
it was naïve to think that the IOC would respect Canada's
human rights policies, regardless of the high-sounding principles of the Olympic Charter.

In 2009, the group took the case to the BC Supreme Court,
arguing that the Winter Olympic program that excluded
women's ski jump events violated the Canadian Charter of
Rights and Freedoms. The judge agreed that VANOC was
subject to the Charter since it was involved in a 'governmental

activity', but rejected the case on a technicality: the IOC had exclusive control over the program, and so VANOC itself had not breached the Charter. An appeal failed on similar grounds, and the Supreme Court of Canada refused to hear the case. Some saw the outcome as a moral victory since the judge had confirmed that the organizing committee was not a private body, and that women's exclusion was discriminatory. However, as always, the real moral of the story was that the Olympic industry, exercising its jurisdictional control over sport disputes through CAS, had the upper hand. The BC appeal court defined an Olympic event as a benefit conferred by the IOC, and not by the Canadian government (Findlay, 2013; Mazzucco & Findlay, 2010; Young, 2010). Interestingly, a 2007 CAS decision had ruled that, although it received government funding, the Canadian Centre for Ethics in Sport was an independent private organization and therefore not subject to the Canadian Charter or the Canadian Human Rights Act (CAS 2007/A/1312). One might therefore ask how the Canadian Centre for Ethics in Sport earned its name.

2.5. CAS'S CLOSED LIST PROBLEM

ICAS is responsible for appointing a closed list of arbitrators, each with renewable four-year terms. The 2004 Code required ICAS to select one-fifth of the arbitrators from those proposed by the IOC, including actual IOC members; Denis Oswald, for example, is an IOC member who has served on many CAS panels. One-fifth of ICAS's membership is selected from qualified persons proposed by IFs, one-fifth by NOCs, one-fifth by those viewed as 'safeguarding the interests of athletes', and the remaining one-fifth independent of the other bodies. In 2016, there were 362 CAS arbitrators on the general list, 92 of whom were also on the football list, and a further 24 were appointed in January 2017.

Critics have identified numerous problems associated with CAS's closed list of arbitrators (see, for example, Cavalieros, 2014; Mangan, 2009; Rigozzi, 2010). Arbitration lawyer Philippe Cavalieros, for example, pointed to the limits it imposes on party autonomy, already restricted by mandatory arbitration; the lack of transparency and subjective criteria used in making the list; a higher risk of repeat appointments and appointment bias; conflict of interest; lack of opportunity for statistical analysis of arbitrators' decisions; no notification of dissenting opinion; ICAS's excessive power; and the politicization of process to become an arbitrator. However, he also noted that parties with limited experience with arbitration because of their cultural backgrounds may benefit from having a closed list of qualified arbitrators, thereby avoiding their tendency 'to appoint arbitrators with whom they enjoy good relations rather than those with strong qualifications.' As a 'halfway' solution, Cavalieros suggested the use of optional lists (Cavalieros, 2014).

The issue of cultural differences is an important one, and CAS supporters claim that many athletes have a better chance of a fair outcome through CAS than through their domestic courts. If this were a common perception among athletes from non-western and/or non-democratic countries, China, for example, one might expect those athletes to be well represented as appellants in CAS cases. With the notable exception of the two Russian teams that were disqualified from the 2016 Rio Olympics, which could be considered a unique situation, there is little evidence from the published decisions that many athletes in this category have brought their appeals to CAS. Furthermore, on the matter of cultural differences, athletes unfamiliar with the arbitration process in general would have to rely on their lawyers to investigate arbitrators' possible lack of independence.

The 2004 edition of the CAS Code included directions for ICAS to consider the matter of distribution when selecting CAS arbitrators, with the IOC, IFs and NOCs each proposing one-fifth of the total, another one-fifth, 'after appropriate consultations, with a view to safeguarding the interests of the athletes', and the remaining one-fifth to be independent of these bodies. On the issue of athletes' interests, no specific organization was mentioned in the 2004 Code, but, in the 2016 amendments, the athletes' commissions of the IOC, IFs and NOCs were listed as bodies that could bring forward names for ICAS's consideration as arbitrators. In terms of eligibility, the Code has long included the following criteria: '[…] appropriate legal training, recognized competence with regard to sports law and/or international arbitration, a good knowledge of sport in general and a good command of at least one CAS working language […]' (English or French). In 2016, in order to encourage eligible athletes to apply for membership, CAS began to organize training for those who had the appropriate legal background but lacked arbitration experience (Mavromati, 2016, p. 40).

In terms of nationality, the numbers are also non-representative. Figures for 2017 showed that Switzerland, presumably because of geographic proximity to CAS, had 29 members, whereas Canada, generally classified as 'a sporting nation', with 36 million residents, had only 14. Australia, another major sporting country but with a relatively small population of 24 million, had 25 CAS arbitrators. Australian IOC member John Coates has served as ICAS president since 2007, and when sports administrator Danni Roche challenged him in the 2017 Australian Olympic Committee (AOC) presidential election, sport leaders raised concerns that Australian interests at the IOC level would be in jeopardy if he were to lose. Hence, it is possible that Coates' leadership and influence may have played a part in Australia's relatively high representation of CAS arbitrators.

In 2014, Coates announced that, with the election of eight new members that year, the 20-member ICAS had for the first time achieved gender equality as well as strengthening its geographic representation (TAS-CAS, 2014). Within the ranks of CAS arbitrators, however, men continue to outnumber women. In terms of age, older white males are over-represented, and arbitrators' ages range from early 40s to 90. Since French and English are the two official languages of the IOC and CAS, it is not surprising to find that France, Canada, the UK, the US, and Australia account for about 130 of the 370 current CAS members (2016 figures). However, only about 15% of English- and French-speaking arbitrators from these western countries are female. Thus, a female athlete is very unlikely to have her case heard by a female arbitrator(s), and a non-English or French-speaking athlete will need to find counsel who speaks their own language as well as English or French, or will have to pay translation costs.

Although no actual changes have appeared in the CAS Code, it seems that selection criteria have been broadened in the last few years, with somewhat less emphasis placed on sport-related backgrounds or experience, and some attempt has been made to appoint arbitrators who did not have direct links to SGBs, a recurring pattern among past members of CAS. Of the 27 new members appointed in 2017, about one-third had no sport content listed in their online profiles, although, interestingly, the four new female members did (TAS-CAS, 2017b).

While the 2004 CAS Code had allowed for individuals within the membership of the IOC, IFs, and NOCs to be proposed to ICAS, later editions were not specific on the question of proportions. They referred only to 'qualified' individuals proposed by those bodies, and did not explicitly extend eligibility to their membership. Nevertheless, several members continue to have dual roles. Since at least 2004 the CAS Code has stated that ICAS members cannot serve as CAS arbitrators or mediators, or as counsel for parties in CAS disputes. Further on the issue of independence, S.11 of the Statutes of ICAS states that a CAS arbitrator 'shall pre-emptively disqualify herself/himself when the subject of a decision is an arbitration procedure in which a sports-related body to which she/he belongs appears as a party or in which a member of the law firm to which she/he belongs is an arbitrator or counsel' (TAS-CAS, 2017c).

It could be argued that this rule would disqualify an IOC member who is also a CAS arbitrator from hearing a dispute that involves the IOC or any IF that governs an Olympic sport. The IOC Member Oath, which includes the commitment 'to serve in *all circumstances* the interests of the IOC' (emphasis added), is a sworn statement that casts doubt on IOC members' ability to serve as impartial CAS arbitrators in disputes where the IOC is a party. Furthermore, since the Olympic Charter names all IFs and NOCs as members of the 'Olympic Movement', an IOC member would also appear to be in conflict of interest if he/she served as a CAS judge in cases involving these parties, in other words, in the majority of CAS appeals.

Despite the potential for conflict of interest, commentators often defend CAS's integrity by referring to the sworn declaration that arbitrators make, 'undertaking to perform their functions in a personal manner, with total objectivity and independence, and in conformity with the provisions of the Code of Sports-Related Arbitration' (see, for example, McLaren, 2001c, 383; Wendt, 2012, p. 182). In other words, it seems to be an article of faith that CAS arbitrators can be trusted to be self-regulating and impartial, despite the fact

that significant numbers had, or continue to have, direct ties
with NOCs, SGBs and even the IOC. As further evidence of
its independence, CAS supporters often cite the few instances
where CAS arbitrators criticized the IOC and/or overturned
IOC decisions (McLaren, 2001c, p. 383). In a 2004 appeal to
CAS, for example, the Australian Olympic Committee
succeeded in challenging an IOC ruling concerning the eligibility of a female kayaker (OG 04/006), and in 2011, a CAS
panel found that Rule 45 of the Olympic Charter violated the
principle of double jeopardy and was unenforceable (CAS
2011/O/2422) (see Chapter 3). According to Rigozzi et al.,
this CAS award was 'the most eloquent example of the
independence of CAS in relation to the IOC' (Rigozzi et al.,
2016, p. 3).

A search of published CAS decisions shows that the IOC
was a party in 56 proceedings in the period 1998−2016, and
respondent in 47 of these. Most appeals were lodged by individual athletes, sometimes in conjunction with their SGB,
while three involved disputes between the IOC and SGBs.
The IOC was appellant in nine cases, all of which were
upheld. Of the cases in which the IOC was respondent, seven
appeals were upheld, five were partially upheld, and 28 were
dismissed. (Three were denied jurisdiction, and one was with-
drawn.) Overall, the odds against a successful outcome for an
individual athlete and/or their SGB were about one in five,
and arguments asserting CAS's independence from the IOC
were not convincingly supported by this evidence, although
the trend only applies to published decisions. WADA's track
record at CAS was somewhat more balanced. WADA was
appellant in 64 cases and respondent in 10; about half of
WADA's appeals were upheld, as were about half of the
appeals by athletes and/or SGBs against WADA, according to
published awards.

Proponents of CAS pointed to the rapidly growing number of cases as a sign of a successful system that athletes trusted (see, for example, Anderson, 2000, p. 126), but generally ignored the fact that forced arbitration gave athletes no other options for the initial stage of dispute resolution. Equally significant, there has been an increase in the number of appeals of CAS awards to SFT, amounting to more than 100 since 2008, although their success rate continues to be close to zero, given the limited procedural grounds for appeal. An analysis of SFT arbitration up to 2007 found that it was 'statistically highly probable' that an appellant would lose their case and would then have to pay costs (Rigozzi, 2010, p. 229).

For those considering appeals to SFT, Rigozzi provided the following advice:

> — *For the counsel to the parties: an analysis of the chances of success and of the costs of a proceedings before the Swiss Supreme Court should induce them to be very prudent in advising an athlete to file an action to set aside or a request for revision of an award.*

> — *For the parties, notably for the athletes: the foregoing makes it clear that the CAS is becoming the only instance where they can assert their rights. (Rigozzi, 2010, p. 265)*

Focusing on the implications for CAS, specifically the need for it to be, and to appear to be, above reproach, Rigozzi concluded: 'This, in turn, highlights the heavy responsibility resting on the shoulders of CAS arbitrators and of CAS as an institution, as well as the real need for a jurisprudence of the highest quality' (Rigozzi, 2010, p. 265).

2.6. SPORT AUTONOMY AND
SPORT SPECIFICITY CHALLENGED

On the issue of internal governance, the IOC's campaign to promote sport autonomy has a history dating back to 1949, when the concept was introduced into the Olympic Charter to promote the autonomy of NOCs, and to resist state interference in sport, most notably on the part of Soviet Bloc countries. Having the power to accept or reject a country's request to participate in the Olympics, the IOC was able to exert indirect pressure on governments. Decades later, in the vastly different geopolitical context of 1992, the Council of Europe agreed that voluntary SGBs had 'the right to establish autonomous decision-making processes within the law.' However, a landmark 1995 European Court of Justice (ECJ) judgement threatened this autonomy, when football player Jean-Marc Bosman successfully challenged FIFA's transfer regulations in relation to the European Economic Community Treaty. Rejecting arguments that football's 'nationality clauses' were justified solely on noneconomic grounds, the court found that they contravened Article 48 of the Treaty, the right to free access to employment within the European Union (EU) community (Chappelet, 2016, p. 17).

A few years later, sport gained some of the immunity from European law that it had been seeking for decades. The Nice Declaration of 2000 confirmed that SGBs in European countries, with 'due regard' for European law, and 'on the basis of a democratic and transparent method of operation… enjoy independence and the right to organize themselves' (cited in Chappelet, 2016, p. 17). The wording did not imply unfettered freedom, but included the condition that European SGBs should exercise their autonomy responsibly vis-à-vis stakeholders and the EU.

In another challenge to the 'sport specificity' principle, two professional athletes whose appeals to lower courts had failed took their case to the ECJ in 2006. They claimed that the IOC's doping rules contravened the European Community's provisions on competition, specifically Article 81, prohibiting practices aimed at 'the prevention, restriction or distortion of competition within the internal market.' CAS had previously upheld FINA's doping decision and the two-year ban on long-distance swimmers David Meca-Medina and Igor Majcen. The European Court of First Instance stated that doping rules were outside the scope of EU law because they had a non-economic objective, but the ECJ ruled that European competition rules did apply to sports rules. Courts could evaluate sports rules in order to determine if the limits and penalties were acceptable and proportionate to their objectives (McArdle & Callery, 2011).

Although the ECJ did not overturn the lower court's judgment, it concluded that 'sporting exception' did not exempt sport from European law, and challenged the false distinction between sporting rules and economic objectives. As McArdle noted, while the case illustrated willingness on the part of the ECJ to acknowledge specialist sport knowledge, its ruling showed that it would exercise appropriate oversight of CAS and similar sport bodies when the rights of EU citizens were at stake (McArdle, 2011, p. 1; McArdle & Callery, 2011).

Putting forward an opposing view on the Meca-Medina case, Gianni Infantino labelled the ECJ's decision 'a step backward for the European sports model and the specificity of sport', lamenting that it 'opened the floodgates' for similar challenges (Infantino, 2006, p. 9). At that time, Infantino headed the Union of European Football Association (UEFA) Legal Affairs and Club Licensing Division; in 2016 he was elected FIFA president after Blatter's suspension.

Infantino claimed that CAS was 'a far more appropriate forum' for sport-related disputes than the ECJ, which he criticized for failing to consider relevant CAS decisions, even though CAS itself did not necessarily refer to its own past awards. In a further comment, Infantino claimed that the timing of the ECJ decision was 'ironic' because European political leaders were currently concerned about 'the special place of sport in the community', and seeking clarity concerning 'sports rules' that were exempt from the EC Treaty. He went on to state that the ECJ appeared 'to have paid not the slightest bit of attention to this *political background*, perhaps […] [the judges] are quite detached from the prevailing *political mood* in Europe' (Infantino, 2006, 10, emphasis added) – ironic, indeed, in light of almost a century of sport leaders' entreaties to keep politics out of sport. Three years later, it was clear that the sport research community fully recognized the intersection of sport and politics, when the 2009 inaugural issue of *International Journal of Sport Policy and Politics* had the EU White Paper as its theme.

2.6.1. Impartiality: SFT Appeals

On the question of CAS panels' impartiality, supporters of specialized sport arbitrators often argued that 'efficiency and expertise would be lost by focusing exclusively on neutrality' (Netzle, 1992, p. 4). As Mangan (2009) observed, although each party's autonomy 'has thus been sacrificed for efficiency', there still remained the option of challenging an arbitrator on the grounds of alleged lack of independence. In the small world of sports law, particularly in Europe, it is not surprising to find situations where appellants to CAS have challenged the independence of counsel or arbitrators. In a 2008 contract dispute before CAS, Jorge Ibarrola, counsel for

FIFA, was alleged to have 'insider' status. Ibarrola had previously served as a clerk on approximately 400 CAS cases. Grounds on which the appellants, two football agents from Argentina, based their appeal to SFT included the claim that the CAS tribunal had been 'illegally composed' or biased. They argued that Ibarrola's close relationship with numerous CAS arbitrators in his previous position exceeded 'normal professional contacts', and that the panel therefore lacked independence. However, CAS rules imposed a time limit of seven days on challenges to arbitrators, and SFT found that the appellants had failed to challenge the CAS panel's composition at the beginning of the proceedings, and had therefore forfeited the right to do so (Alleged illegal composition, 2008). Thus, SFT avoided dealing with the appellants' allegation of lack of independence.

Somewhat similar to the argument in the Ibarrola case was a 2012 appeal before SFT, in which appellants again claimed that CAS was not 'an independent tribunal in doping matters but an indirect body of all the federations interested in the outcome' of their dispute. Unfortunately for the appellants, the SFT panel found that they had neglected to raise the claim of 'irregular composition' of the CAS panel within the time limits, and dismissed the appeal (Dismissal... jurisdiction, 2012).

Another unsuccessful appeal to SFT involved a doping dispute. The appellant sought to differentiate between FIFA's anti-doping rules and those of the Cyprus Football Association, claiming that the latter referred only to the 'substantive' rules and did not create CAS jurisdiction. The SFT decision of April 18, 2011 made several references to the importance of 'the international fight against doping', in view of which they found the appellant's argument 'unpersuasive' (SFT 4A_640/2010). Like CAS and WADA, SFT viewed individual sanctions as a useful deterrent to others in the global fight against doping. However, Charles Poncet, Swiss arbitrator and commentator, with Despina Mavromati, on SFT awards at <swissarbitrationdecisions.com>, offered muted support for that particular decision. He described the appellant's argument as 'well-reasoned' and found the court's decision, which confirmed CAS's jurisdiction and the importance of anti-doping, to be resting on 'at times somewhat thin references' (Dismissal… anti-doping, 2011).

For the most part, SFT did not offer appellants any real hope of success. As the Swiss arbitration commentators explained, SFT has 'well-known reticence to overturn an award on its merits unless the appellant establishes a very strong case – as opposed to issues of jurisdiction, where the review is more detailed and the Court's reluctance to interfere less manifest' (Allegedly infra petita award, 2009). One critic described the SFT as simply providing 'quality assurance for CAS decisions', but pointed out that if needed, national courts 'could provide a fundamental safeguard for the members and athletes governed by sports organizations' (Reilly, 2012, p. 80). With some notable exceptions in European courts, discussed below, there is little evidence that this 'safeguard' is effective.

In several introductory notes on Swiss arbitration decisions, commentators appeared to take a dim view of repeated attempts to challenge CAS decisions, noting on more than one occasion that CAS 'has become the main "provider" of appeals' to SFT, many of which did not justify such an appeal, and did not contribute new or interesting opinions to the field of international arbitration (Judicial review, 2010). In fact, one of their commentaries was titled 'Another hopeless sport-related appeal…', a case that cost the appellant CHF 12,000 (about US$12,400) (SFT 4A_568/2015). Taking a different perspective, Rigozzi (2010, p. 264) identified 'the threat to the long-term autonomy of arbitration' if there were a public perception that there was 'no real possibility of setting aside awards.' Indeed, more than 100 mostly unsuccessful appeals to SFT over about a 20-year period would contribute to this perception of the futility, as well as the expense, of doing so.

2.6.2. Benfica and Matuzalem

It was not until 2010 that SFT first set aside a 2004 CAS award on the basis of a violation of procedural public policy. That case involved a dispute between Benfica and Atletico football clubs, after Benfica sought compensation for a player who had trained with them before transferring to Atletico. In 2002, FIFA granted compensation to Benfica, but in a 2004 judgement, the Zurich Commercial Court found that FIFA's transfer regulations violated Swiss and European competition law. In 2009, Atletico appealed to CAS, the CAS panel disregarded the Zurich court judgement, and granted compensation to Benfica. Finally, in 2010, SFT rejected the CAS decision on the grounds that it violated public policy, specifically the principle of *res judicata* (where the same matter had already been decided by a judicial body) (Setting aside of award, 2010).

Two years later, the landmark Matuzalem case marked the first time that SFT annulled a CAS award on the basis of substantive as well as procedural law. The CAS decision had upheld FIFA's banning of the Brazilian football player from all competition until he paid compensation totaling more than EUR11.8m to his former club for breach of contract (Valloni & Pachmann, 2012). FIFA, with its headquarters in Switzerland, is subject to the Swiss Federal Constitution, as well as the Swiss Private International Law Act. As the SFT decision noted, the Constitution guarantees the right to personal and economic freedom: 'the right to choose a profession freely and to access an occupational activity freely' (SFT 4A_558/2011, 4.3.1). Furthermore, that right cannot be curtailed by state or private persons and 'a person may not legally pledge to relinquish his freedom entirely.' Therefore, the SFT found that the CAS award that upheld FIFA's 'unlimited occupational ban' on Matuzalem was 'an obvious and grave violation of privacy and is contrary to public policy' (4.3.5).

2.7. SPORT EXCEPTIONALISM AND EU LAW

Following the Bosman and Meca-Medina decisions, sports organizations redoubled their efforts to establish the autonomy of sport. For their part, the European Commission's Sport Unit, headed by Michal Krejza, conducted a two-year consultation, resulting in the 2007 EU White Paper on Sport. Commenting on the report, CAS arbitrator Ian Blackshaw noted that FIFA and other IFs would be disappointed in its contents, specifically the continued distinction between 'the business/economic and the social sides of sport', since several IFs had been lobbying for 'sport specificity' and exemption from EU law for years (Blackshaw, 2007, p. 88). Another commentator, Jonathon Hill, asked whether sport rules were 'under attack', since the White Paper had reiterated the Meca-Medina decision 'that dismissed the notion of "purely sporting rules" as irrelevant for the question of the applicability of EU competition rules to the sport sector' (Hill, 2009, 261). He further suggested that the White Paper might represent a 'step backwards for specificity', but acknowledged that it did include a list of sport-related rules — 'rules of the game', selection criteria, anti-doping rules, and others — that were unlikely to violate the EC Treaty's competition rules (Hill, 2009, pp. 253, 261).

Several years later, an implicit warning in a 2015 CAS award appeared to recognize this reality. Two male athletes had appealed the suspensions imposed on them by the international volleyball federation, in part on the grounds that the 'flawed' disciplinary proceedings did not respect due process; furthermore, they called for 'deep reform' of the organization. The sole arbitrator, Alasdair Bell, was also Director of Legal Affairs at UEFA. Noting that CAS only revised a sanction if it were clearly inappropriate or wrong, Bell added his opinion that CAS could certainly comment, 'in circumstances that might be deemed useful and appropriate, on the manner in which sports judicial bodies discharge their given tasks, in particular, as regards matters of due process' (CAS 2015/A/4095, S.69). In relation to the provisions of the European Convention on Human Rights (ECHR), Bell noted that they did not apply to federations' disciplinary bodies, which were not 'tribunals', but went on to state that it might be 'a useful practical exercise to consider whether guarantees afforded under the ECHR have been respected. This is also against the background of any *further possible appeal* of a CAS Award' to the SFT (s. 73, emphasis added). On the same issue, the decision cited the views of another CAS arbitrator, Ulrich Haas:

> *In proceedings relating to arbitration, the state courts are under a duty to guarantee that the inalienable values of the ECHR that form part of public policy ('ordre public') are observed. From this it follows that the arbitral tribunals like the CAS are at least indirectly bound by this system of values under ECHR. (CAS 2015/A/4095, s. 73)*

The IOC and CAS rightly saw the Meca-Medina decision as a threat to their independence. In fact, as an IOC news release indignantly announced, 'since 2006 some *ten serious interferences* in sports' structures and regulations' had been reported, a clear indication, in the IOC's view, of the need to 'protect its independence not only from governments but also from commercial partners and other bodies' (IOC, 2008, emphasis added). In February 2008, the IOC's seminar on the autonomy of the Olympic movement adopted a resolution that reflected, on paper at least, their belief that good governance was 'the fundamental basis to secure the Autonomy of Olympic and Sports Organizations.' Members subsequently developed a set of 'basic universal principles' to achieve good governance, presumably in an attempt to demonstrate that they had earned this autonomy (IOC, 2008).

The 2011 version of the Olympic Charter, Fundamental Principle 5, entrenched the related principles of autonomy and good governance. In a 2013 speech to the UN, IOC president Thomas Bach claimed that sport could only promote the 'global ethic' of fair play, tolerance and friendship if it had 'responsible autonomy.' 'Politics must respect this sporting autonomy', he insisted, and concluded with a typical flourish of Olympic industry entitlement. Sport, he proclaimed, would respect some national laws but not others – specifically, any that were 'targeted against sport and its organizations alone, sometimes for chiefly political reasons' (Bach, 2013, p. 3). It is difficult to contemplate how a threat to ignore inconvenient national laws would be received in any other context. Yet, sport exceptionalism appears to trump all other considerations.

As the authors of the 2013 Sport Governance Observer report aptly observed, if SGBs wanted legal certainty regarding EU law and were concerned about repeated challenges to their internal rules, they should do more to empower stakeholders to have a vote, or at least a voice, in determining those rules. Instead of demanding special treatment for sport, SGBs need to become more accountable, democratic and transparent, thereby reducing the problem of disempowered and dissatisfied athletes who turn to European courts for justice (Geeraert et al., 2013, p. 205).

Legal scholars' predictions that the EU would support citizens' rights were borne out in a 2017 decision that again invoked EU competition rules, this time in a case against the International Skating Union (ISU). The case began in 2015 when two Dutch speed skaters, Mark Tuitert and Niels Kerstholt, filed a complaint with the European Commission (EC) concerning ISU penalties, including life bans on athletes who participated in unauthorized events. The EC decision of December 2017 found that ISU breached EU antitrust law (restrictive business practices), and required that it change the rules within 90 days to allow professional skaters to compete in non-ISU events. The commissioner stated that, to be compatible with EU law, sporting rules must pursue legitimate sporting objectives and restrictions must be 'inherent and proportionate', not, as in the ISU case, 'to enable the ISU to pursue its own commercial interests.' Athletes should not face penalties and be deprived of earning additional income for participating in other events during the relatively short duration of their speed skating careers. Like earlier decisions, the EC differentiated between sporting objectives – protecting health, safety and integrity of competitions – and commercial objectives that served to stop business rivals from organizing sporting events (Antitrust, 2017). Predictably, Bach expressed concern about 'certain interpretations' of EU law invoking 'the social value of sport', which he emphasized should not be equated with 'commercial sport business' (IOC, 2017b). Yet, as the record shows, when it serves the interests of Olympic industry players, the 'social value' takes a distant second place to profits (Lenskyj, 2000, 2002, 2008).

2.8. CONCLUSION

The previous discussion has examined the history of CAS in
relation to the broader movement to establish sport autonomy,
as well as providing details of significant SFT decisions that
have protected the rights of individual athletes. Like other
commentators, I have referred to these as *landmark* decisions,
and yet, in hindsight, it appears that such cases have not sub-
stantively changed the course of CAS's history, but have
merely prompted superficial changes to the CAS Code and the
Olympic Charter. While legal challenges may benefit only individual athletes or teams, economic threats to the Olympic
industry clearly carry more weight. With ever-decreasing numbers of bid cities vying to host future Olympics, the industry
and its leaders may be forced to pay greater attention to issues
of athletes' rights and social justice, if for no other reason than
to protect the Olympic brand from further disrepute, just as
the global fight against doping in sport, discussed in the following chapters, shares the same goal.

PART II

CHAPTER 3

THE WAR ON DOPING

Doping is universally viewed as the most serious problem confronting high performance sport and a major threat to its global reputation and integrity. Arguably more important is the threat that doping poses to sport's credibility and appeal to commercial sponsors, and the subsequent damage to Olympic industry brands. In sport circles, the demonization of doping and those who dope is taken as a self-evident truth, and it is not surprising to find that more CAS appeals involve doping than the other major categories of eligibility, contract, transfer, discipline, nationality and governance.

For decades, the broad subject of doping in sport has attracted an extensive body of scholarly and popular literature that far exceeds most other sport-related topics. In addition to reviewing relevant analyses in law and sport sciences literature, the following discussion will challenge the widely accepted premise that the 'fight against doping' is fully justified. The threat that over-zealous anti-doping campaigns and subsequent CAS decisions pose to athletes' rights will be exposed, with a particular focus on the ways in which the variables of gender and 'race'/ethnicity are played out.

Although generally considered to be underestimations of doping prevalence, statistics provided by WADA's annual Anti-Doping Rule Violations Reports (ADRV) show that a clear majority of ADRVs come from male athletes. Figures for 2013 showed about 80% of the 1,287 ADRV samples were from men, and in 2014 and 2015, 79% were from male athletes. Possible explanations for the dramatic gender differences include greater media attention, enhanced career opportunities, and more lucrative sponsorships flowing from international sporting success. In short, men may risk more to gain more. In terms of detection, men have an advantage, since the physical changes that testosterone derivatives produce are compatible with hegemonic masculinities, whereas similar changes in women are likely to attract more scrutiny.

The few research studies that examine gender differences in doping identified a number of psychological as well as physiological factors that had a greater deterrent effect on women than on men. These included a guilty conscience, unfairness to other athletes, illegality, suspension, unnatural physical changes, reduced fertility, and the risk of media exposure and embarrassment (Overbye, Knudsen, & Pfister, 2013). Reviewing research on gender differences dating back to 2011, Mazanov (2016) found that the use of supplements and illicit drugs was higher among male than female athletes, while prescription drugs and supplements for diet or health reasons were more likely to be used by females.

3.1. NATIONALISM

Sport has long been termed a war without weapons, and Olympic sport lends itself to wars of rhetoric as well as highly symbolic, internationally televised victories in the sporting arena. It is difficult for politicians and sports leaders to win this war if their country's sporting achievements are tainted by allegations of doping. Not only should doping be exposed and punished, according to this reasoning, but it must also be seen to be exposed and punished. Mainstream media play a key role in these processes, often with a cavalier disregard for the facts.

In specific historical contexts — the Cold War, China's economic ascendancy, and Putin's Russia, for example — international posturing about doping in sport serves to shame and blame 'other' nations' athletes for their 'unbelievable' (drug-assisted) performances. In the 1970s, the German Democratic Republic's state-ordered doping program was widely viewed as evidence of the evils of Communism. Similarly, in the 1980s and 1990s, China became the subject of scrutiny following the unexpected winning performances of Chinese athletes, especially swimmers, in international competition, while, since 2016, Russian athletes have been the focus of global attention and censure. Meanwhile, athletes from purportedly 'clean' countries may evade detection.

At the 2012 London Olympics, as doping suspicions continued to target Chinese swimmers, 16-year-old Ye Shiwen won the 200 m and 400 m individual medley (IM) events. In the final freestyle lap of the 400 m event, she swam faster than the top male swimmer, American Ryan Lochte. Veteran American swim coach John Leonard called Shiwen's performance 'unbelievable,' 'an outrageous performance,' and 'suspicious,' while other coaches and swimmers added their own allegations. Claiming that Shiwen had failed to demonstrate 'a normal improvement curve,' Leonard pronounced: '[...] a woman does not out-swim the fastest man in the world in the back quarter of a 400m IM that is otherwise quite ordinary. It just doesn't happen' (quoted in Bull, 2012). In other words, Shiwen was guilty of doping or she was not a 'real' woman.

(According to published sources, Shiwen has not failed any doping tests to date.)

3.2. GLOBAL ANTI-DOPING EFFORTS

It is widely argued in sport circles that consistent universal definitions of banned substances must be applied if the global fight against doping is to be won. The World Anti-Doping Agency (WADA) was established in 1999 under the leadership of IOC vice president Richard Pound, and the WADA Code came into force in 2004, with CAS serving as the body responsible for final resolution of doping disputes. For their part, CAS panels have no role in establishing anti-doping rules and policies; they merely enforce the rules on behalf of WADA by hearing appeals. Although most appellants are individual athletes or teams, WADA itself uses the services of CAS to appeal what it considers an inadequate penalty determined by a national sports body, or to challenge an inadequate testing program or laboratory in a non-compliant country. WADA was a party in 74 published CAS cases between 1986 and 2016, 64 as appellant and 10 as respondent. Of WADA's appeals, 31 were upheld and 20 partially upheld, thereby giving WADA, and WADA's lawyers, a fairly high success rate at CAS.

There have been a few instances where CAS panels have rebuked IFs or other sports bodies for their failure to communicate doping regulations clearly, or when their rules and sanctions exceed those of the WADA Code, but they generally reserved their strongest language for athletes. Admittedly, some athletes resorted to bizarre defenses in their attempts to reduce or eliminate doping-related suspensions, blaming, among other sources, their mothers, their sex partners, menstrual bleeding, contaminated food or water, and polluted ocean water. A closer examination of CAS doping decisions reveals many of the same problems of inconsistency and unpredictability found in non-doping matters.

Unlike many individual appellants, WADA has sufficient resources to access highly experienced and successful counsel to represent it before CAS. Despite the 'stacked decks' advantage, however, it appears that, overall, WADA is losing the war. Innocent athletes have been penalized, and guilty parties have escaped punishment (Boye et al., 2017; Greene, 2017). As sport scholars Moller and Dimeo demonstrated in their case study of cycling, 'sport is essentially deteriorating under the current anti-doping campaign executed by an un-coordinated alliance between the WADA, law enforcement authorities, sports organizers and the media' (Moller & Dimeo, 2014, p. 260). They proposed an end to this 'moral crusade' that shows little sign of success. Although WADA interpreted the increase in (detected) doping offenses in 2015 compared to 2014 as evidence of a greater focus on 'investigation, intelligence gathering and whistleblowing' (WADA, 2017b), the change could equally represent an increase in the real incidence of doping.

It is clear that, from WADA's perspective, eternal vigilance is the key to winning the war against doping. In addition to an ever-increasing list of banned substances, WADA's 2004 introduction of the *Whereabouts* regulation added another layer to its anti-doping campaign. Elite athletes were required to enter details of their whereabouts, on a daily basis, into WADA's online Administration and Management System (or by telephone) to help officials conduct out-of-competition random testing. A 2015 change to WADA's Code introduced uniform rules for all countries and sport for breaches of the *Whereabouts* rules: a standard two-year sanction and a 'three strikes in 12-months' rule for missed tests (WADA, 2015).

3.3. ANTI-DOPING DISCOURSE

A discourse analysis that identifies how language functions to support WADA's hegemony provides a useful starting point. Sport scholar Scott Jedlicka (2014) subjected the 2007 WADA Code to a detailed investigation, posing two key questions: 'What is produced by this language?' and 'Who or what benefits from (or is harmed) by this?' Of particular relevance to this discussion is his elaboration of the ways in which the Code's language has created 'an extralegal environment' compatible with WADA's unfettered global control over doping and dopers in sport. Ironically, the signatories to WADA who were responsible for giving it that power in the first place now found themselves subject to it, a situation that produced a number of internal debates over governance (discussed below).

The following section from the 2007 WADA Code, cited by Jedlicka (pp. 436—437) unequivocally establishes the full extent of WADA's jurisdiction and authority while perfectly exemplifying sport exceptionalism — 'a separate world' that excludes athletes from 'the rights and protections' offered by traditional legal systems:

> *These sport-specific rules and procedures aimed at enforcing anti-doping rules in a global and harmonized way are distinct in nature from and are, therefore, not intended to be subject to or limited by any national requirements and legal standards applicable to criminal proceedings or employment matters. When reviewing the facts and the law of a given case, all courts, arbitral hearing panels and other adjudicating bodies should be aware and respect the distinct nature of the anti-doping rules in the Code and the fact that those rules represent the*

> *consensus of a broad spectrum of stakeholders*
> *around the world with an interest in fair sport.*
> *(Introduction, p. 18, cited in Jedlicka, 2014,*
> *pp. 435–436)*

The explicit and inevitable invoking of the moral high ground and references to those with 'an interest in fair sport' effectively renders morally suspect anyone who dares to dissent, as well as issuing a stern warning to errant judges and arbitrators who are not associated with CAS to keep out of the sport business. As Lopez and others have pointed out, anti-doping rhetoric reflects a moral panic based on a pseudo-Christian value system, 'with its references to crusades, heretics, sinners, repentants, cleanliness and purification' (Lopez, 2010, p. 14).

In anti-doping rhetoric, the term 'clean athletes' is particularly revealing since its opposite, 'unclean/dirty,' denotes serious physical and moral deficits. In a 2017 interview, UK heptathlete Kelly Sotherton went beyond the symbolism of 'clean' to reject the actual bronze medal that she was awarded following the disqualification of two former medalists, one from Russia and the other from Ukraine. She claimed that the medal itself was 'dirty and tainted' because it had been worn by a doping athlete (Kelly Sotherton, 2017). Similarly endorsing the paramount importance of 'clean sport,' but perhaps without considering the full implications of his words, UK boxer Tyson Fury defended himself against doping charges in 2017 by stating: 'Of all the things I've been called – a bigot, a sexist, a homophobe – I may have been those things but the one thing I'm not is a drug cheat... that's *the worst* a sportsman can be' (Tyson Fury, 2017, emphasis added).

On the role of CAS, Jedlicka observed that, although it might help athletes to appeal unfair WADA decisions, it merely monitors enforcement rather than evaluates WADA's rules. The WADA Code dictates that athletes cannot challenge WADA's determination of its Prohibited List or argue that a substance or method fails to meet WADA's three criteria for inclusion on the list: potential for enhancement, health risk, and violation of the spirit of sport (Jedlicka, 2012, pp. 438–439).

While performance-enhancing function and health risks can, to some extent, be established scientifically (although not without extensive disagreement and debate), the 'spirit of sport' is entirely subjective and narrowly defined to support so-called Olympic ideals. First introduced in the 2003 version of the WADA Code, 'the spirit of sport' clause, as sport scholar Ian Ritchie demonstrated, reflected policymakers' interest in promoting a 'values-based' image, while at the same time inserting a blanket provision to cover new drugs or methods not named in existing codes (Ritchie, 2013, p. 198).

Among the components of 'the spirit of sport' identified in WADA's 'Fundamental Rationale' are 'Ethics, fair play and honesty; Health; Excellence in performance; Character and education; Fun and joy; Teamwork; Dedication and commitment; Respect for rules and laws; Respect for self and other participants; Courage; Community and solidarity' (WADA, 2015, p. 14). Clearly these are culturally specific, gendered concepts that invoke the Modern Olympics' foundational 'values' and, beyond that, the shadow of the Ancient Greek warrior/athlete/hero.

The 120-year hegemony of the Modern Olympics has entrenched one expression of human movement – defined as sport – to the exclusion of all others. The achievement sport model, as German sociologist Henning Eichberg explained, supplanted the fitness model and the body achievement model, neither of which was compatible with the 'global sportification of physical activities' (Eichberg, 1998, 2004; Suchet, Jorand, & Tuppen, 2010, p. 577). This global

sportifying/unifying/colonizing project has been a key function of the Olympic industry from the start, as exemplified
by founder Coubertin's proposal to hold the first African
Games in 1923 along with his prediction that 'sport will
conquer Africa' (Suchet et al., 2010; see also Lenskyj, 2013,
chapter 2). According to this line of thinking, a quantifiable
result is an essential component of sport – hence the
faster/higher/stronger principle of the Olympics. As Lopez
explained, the nature of sport itself is the driving social force
behind biomedical experimentation, given 'its inexorable tendency towards hierarchy, performance and victory' (Lopez,
2010, p. 14).

One might imagine, somewhat idealistically, a different
view of biomedicine if the male-defined 'faster/higher/stron-
ger' model of Olympic sport had not shaped all branches of
physical activity in western countries and beyond. If grace
and flexibility had been valued over record-breaking, and if
lifelong health and enjoyment mattered more than beating
one's opponent, biomedicine would promote these values,
rather than subverting them.

A 'normative discourse of sport' serves to shore up
WADA's generally unchallenged assumption that sport is, by
definition, 'pure' and free of performance-enhancing drugs,
although some sport scholars, Beamish and Ritchie (2006),
for example, demonstrated how doping was mostly unchallenged throughout the early decades of international sporting
competition. In other words, the WADA Code was on thin ice
when it equated anti-doping rules with competition rules.
While the rules of the game are constitutive of sport, anti-
doping rules are not: they are imposed and regulative
(Jedlicka, 2014, p. 437). Despite WADA's best efforts to reach
back into the past to test samples, rewrite record books, and
retract medals, sport is defined by the rules of the game, and
not by any specific iteration of the WADA Code.

3.4. LEGALIZED DOPING?

In 1996, Australian sport scholars Doug Booth and Colin Tatz argued that performance-enhancing drugs should be legalized to help equalize opportunities. Writing an opinion piece in the monthly magazine, *Inside Sport*, they pointed to a recent Australian Senate inquiry into doping that had taken a broader view, identifying inequalities in funding, facilities and training as key factors contributing to the 'uneven playing field' (Booth & Tatz, 1995, p. 14). Views like these foreshadowed the 'pharmaceutical heretic' position that has gained currency since that time − the argument that performance-enhancing drugs should be regulated rather than banned (Savulescu, Foddy, & Clayton, 2004).

Because *Inside Sport* took a strong editorial stance against doping, it printed a disclaimer along with the Booth and Tatz article. Included in the magazine's male-oriented and overtly sexist content were countless articles based on doping suspicions as well as perceived gender transgressions of athletes from Communist or former Communist countries. The article titled 'China's Great Wall of Lies' (Stringer, 1995), included photos of female swimmers that appear to have been digitally enhanced to distort their muscular upper bodies, when compared to other images of these women in the same timeframe (Jarratt, 1995; Lenskyj, 1998).

In the twenty-first century, with the so-called 'fight against doping' escalating on all fronts, it became the target of growing criticism in mainstream and academic sources. In a 2013 online opinion piece titled 'May the best meds win,' former US track and field CEO Doug Logan claimed that this 'war' was both hypocritical and unwinnable. As he argued, athletes who can afford the costs are already benefitting from technological, medical and training advances including altitude training, hyperbaric chambers, access to elite training facilities, and the support of numerous medical and rehabilitation experts, so why not steroids? 'Civilians' are prescribed steroids to speed up recovery from injuries, and Viagra is arguably 'the greatest performance enhancer of them all,' as Logan pointed out (Logan, 2013).

A 2016 *Vice Sports* article on the same topic included interviews with Logan and Don Catlin, a former drug testing investigator who had developed the testosterone/epitestosterone (T/E) test (see Chapter 4). The journalist explained how 'a small group of heretics' including Logan and some academic commentators were challenging conventional wisdom about doping. They argued that the war on doping had imposed 'more harm than good: wasting money, retarding medicine, fostering corruption, and trampling on athletes' rights and dignity while failing to protect their health.' A 'safer, rational and arguably more honest' solution would be 'to permit, study, and regulate the drug use that already happens regardless of the rules' (Hruby, 2016).

From a different but compatible perspective, some critics have proposed the harm reduction model. Proven to be an effective approach to recreational drug use, it may prove to be a viable alternative to WADA's demonstrably unsuccessful 'punishment, zero tolerance and abstinence' approach by offering 'athlete autonomy, agency and safety' through regulatory measures that lessen the harm to participants. Harm reduction advocates emphasize peer education and concern for athletes' rights, privacy, and long-term health, rather than the sport/entertainment industry's current preoccupation with 'short-term brand equity and credibility that might be tarnished by a drug use or drug trafficking incident' (Smith & Stewart, 2015, p. 58).

3.5. LOW DETECTION, HIGH SURVEILLANCE

In a critique of the 2015 changes to the WADA Code, Dimeo pointed to the career-ending consequences of the new four-year ban that replaced the former two-year suspension for those found using a drug, tampering with a sample, or helping others to dope. Regardless, the usual detection rate of only about 2% of those tested remains 'a huge underrepresentation' of the true extent of doping, which is estimated to be in the range of 10–20% depending on other factors, including the sport and the country (Dimeo, 2014). More recent research estimated the range to be 14–39% (de Hon, Kuipers, & van Bottenburg, 2015), and a WADA-commissioned study of athletes at the 2011 IAAF World Championships and 2011 Pan-Arab Games, based on a 'randomized response technique' that guaranteed anonymity, found the doping rate to be 43.6% and 70.1%, respectively (Ulrich et al., 2018).

It was surprising that these 'concerning and disappointing statistics,' as UK Anti-Doping termed them, ever appeared in a scientific journal, given the IAAF's objections and concerted efforts to block publication. It had expressed 'serious reservations as to the interpretation of the result made by the research group,' but these concerns were not substantiated. A full account can be found on <sportintegrity.com>, including original communications that the researchers sent to the Chair of the Culture, Media and Sport Committee, House of Commons, a move that prompted that committee to publish the study in full under parliamentary privilege (Brown, 2017) – yet another example of a failed attempt to keep negative publicity 'inside the family of sport.'

There is little doubt that most doping goes undetected. To achieve these less than stellar detection rates, WADA subjects athletes to an excessive level of monitoring and surveillance, as Dimeo described it, 'much like newly released prisoners or convicted sex offenders,' as well as the 'indignities of urinating in front of a stranger.' Dimeo proposed a more preventative approach, one that included greater athlete involvement in policy-making, improved education, and a focus on non-compliant organizations and countries rather than on individuals (Dimeo, 2014).

Ever-escalating surveillance appears to be an article of faith in the war on doping. On October 11, 2017, Mike Miller, CEO of the World Olympics Association, proposed the use of microchip implants similar to those used to track domestic animals. Responding to privacy concerns, he claimed: 'sport is a club and people don't have to join the club ... if they can't follow the rules' (quoted in Best, 2017). (In fact, the Olympic Charter calls sport participation a *right*, not a club.) Coincidentally, two days earlier, after an Australian swimmer had received a 12-month ban for missing three doping tests, I had expressed my view on Twitter: 'Whereabouts system is unfair = over-the-top surveillance – how about electronic tracking systems, WADA?' Obviously, as I explained in a follow-up tweet, I was only joking.

In a further example of the extremes contemplated by the warriors in this war, in 2017 the IOC funded a project at the University of South Australia, in which researchers in the field of 'experimental economics' would investigate the effectiveness of a 'financial disincentive' plan to deter doping. Athletes would be required to deposit some of their income in a pension plan, and would gain access to these funds after their retirement only if they had a clean doping record. It is difficult to contemplate how such a proposal would be received in any other business or workplace – that is, the idea of an employer threatening to withhold an employee's pension for offenses that may not have involved any illegal substances or criminal charges (Anti-doping study, 2017). That a project based on this premise was even funded provides ample evidence of the extreme interventions into athletes' lives that the Olympic industry considers itself entitled to make.

3.6. STRICT LIABILITY AND THE CRIMINALIZATION
OF DOPING

A controversial aspect of CAS's approach to doping lies in the
presumption of guilt whenever a banned substance is found.
Numerous legal scholars have critiqued the strict liability principle that CAS applies (see, for example, Geeraets, 2017; Kane,
2003; Oschutz, 2002; Schneider, 2004; Straubel, 2005). CAS
and Ad Hoc Division arbitrators do not take subjective elements such as intent, negligence or involuntariness into
account in establishing guilt. Instead, they rely solely on the
finding of a banned substance in an athlete's test results,
regardless of explanations offered for its presence. In the words
of one CAS panel, 'the only decisive thing is that he or she
actually (or potentially) had an unfair advantage,' and 'from
the point of view of other athletes,' intentionality is irrelevant
(CAS 2010/A/2230). In general, CAS arbitrators only consider
intentionality and proportionality when imposing sanctions
(McLaren, 1998, p. 7; Oschutz, 2002, pp. 699–700).

The tension between deterrence and justice underlies much
of WADA's and CAS's fight against doping. Perhaps protest-
ing too much, numerous CAS panels have emphasized that
their goal was not to punish the athlete, but to serve the
greater good. The strict liability principle, they claimed, 'which
at first sight might appear unfair to one athlete may on
mature consideration be justified as fair to athletes as a
whole' (CAS 2001/A/337; see also CAS 2007/A/1312). When
disqualifying past results achieved by athletes who have
doped, CAS panels have asserted that their 'main purpose…
is not to punish the transgressor, but rather to correct any
unfair advantage and remove any tainted performances from
the record' (CAS 2017/O/5039). If estimates of undetected
doping are even close to accurate, the cleansing of 'tainted'
records promises to be a Sisyphean task.

On the question of unfairness, as Oschutz noted, CAS panels have asserted that 'the higher principles and practical objectives of the fight against doping' amply justify the strict liability principle (Oschutz, 2002, pp. 691, 687). WADA's and CAS's application of the 'strict liability' principle appears to be at odds with the presumption of innocence in common law, although the Swiss Federal Tribunal has upheld the principle.

As legal scholar Klaus Wolf pointed out, despite its commitment to 'the fight against doping' and its self-proclaimed function as 'private law-maker and judge,' WADA focuses primarily on the athletes themselves, and lacks the basic tools required to uncover 'the cheats behind the cheats' (Wolf, 2014, pp. 290, 298). Wolf proposed a number of government interventions, in the form of phone taps, authorized searches, and confiscation of drugs to address the global drug trade and its suspected links to organized crime. In the Lance Armstrong case, for example, the FBI participated in the doping investigation. Even at the time of Wolf's proposal, there was evidence of governments having already joined in 'the fight.' Several western countries had criminalized trafficking, possession, and use or administration of steroids through non-sport-specific legislation. By 2013, more than half of the EU countries had enacted sport-specific laws that implemented the 2005 UNESCO Anti-Doping Convention. Between 2000 and 2006, Italy, France, and Austria introduced sport-specific legislation that criminalized offenses involving WADA Code's list of prohibited substances and methods, and by 2013, a small number of convicted athletes, coaches and managers had received prison sentences (Murphy, 2013).

As further evidence of the success of 'sport exceptionalism' arguments, none of these initiatives appear to have prompted human rights organizations to voice concerns about the threat to athletes' rights and the potential for innocent athletes or support personnel to be prosecuted and punished. In fact, in 2018, the European Court of Human Rights upheld the legality of WADA's *Whereabouts* requirement. In proceedings that began in 2010, a number of European sports organizations and individual players had claimed that this requirement violated Article 8 of European Convention on Human Rights, which protected the right to respect for private and family life. The ECHR decision stated that 'public interest grounds' justified such restrictions, and that their removal 'would be at odds with the European and international consensus' concerning the necessity for random testing in fighting 'the scourge' of doping. It noted the prime importance of the 'protection of health' of professional athletes, whose doping would also 'dangerously' encourage amateurs and 'especially young people to follow suit' (Doping control, 2018) – a rationale that invoked 'role model' and 'greater good' arguments. In addition, it warned of negative impacts on spectators, who they claimed 'legitimately expected' fair competition, an implied reference to the threat to the commercial success of professional sport if players were doping.

In October 2017, prompted by legislation enacted in other European countries, the UK Department for Digital, Culture, Media and Sport (2017) released its *Review of Criminalisation of Doping in Sport.* The report concluded that, while improvements in doping control and educational campaigns were needed, changes to criminal law would be 'disproportionate.' Significantly, the reasons underlying the rejection of these changes were pragmatic rather than ethical. Clearly reflecting the views of sports governing bodies and anti-doping authorities, the authors pointed to the disadvantages of criminal courts, compared to regulatory or disciplinary proceedings. Problems included the time-consuming process of establishing guilt 'beyond reasonable doubt' and the lower financial penalties available in criminal court.

Further, it was noted that, in criminal proceedings, strict liability was insufficient, intent would need to be shown, and
appeals were likely to increase. Police priorities and rules
guiding prosecutors' responsibilities would further impede
investigations (Department, 2017, S. 13). In short, this
government-sponsored review reinforced sport leaders' longstanding goal of keeping disputes out of the courts and 'in
the family of sport.'

Several years earlier, in Australia, there had been strong
opposition to the proposed Australian Sports Anti-Doping
Authority (ASADA) Amendment Bill of 2013 that expanded
on ASADA's 2006 bill. The 2013 amendment would have
given ASADA the following enhanced powers:

> [...] to issue a disclosure notice to compel persons to
> attend an interview with an investigator and to
> produce information and documents or things
> relevant to the administration of the National Anti-
> Doping Scheme; impose penalties [up to $5100 per
> day] for failing to comply with a disclosure notice
> [...] [and] enable Australia Post to share information
> with ASADA. (Australian Sports, 2013)

The original version of the Amendment Bill threatened the
individual's privilege against self-incrimination ('right to
silence'), but this provision was removed following objections
by the Green Party, without whose support the government
would have had insufficient votes. As commentators on the
Mondaq Law website observed, it was an 'interesting reflection' on Australia's view of athletes and sport for the legisla-
ture even to have considered abrogating privilege against
self-incrimination (Giles & Loeliger, 2013; see also Hickie,
2016, pp. 47–48). More than simply 'interesting,' I would
argue, since to do so would have been a particularly

egregious example of sport exceptionalism. As Giles and Loeliger explained:

> *[the right to silence is] [...] one of the core principles of our criminal justice system and a fundamental human right [...] Abrogation of that privilege would have subjected athletes and support persons to a higher threshold [...] than individuals suspected of criminal offences'. (Giles & Loeliger, 2013)*

Brendan Schwab, founder of Australian Athletes' Alliance, and, more recently, World Players' Association, expressed serious concerns about the terms of the original bill, as well as the punitive rhetoric of sport leaders like Australian IOC member John Coates:

> *The whole concept that athletes would face a criminal penalty for a breach of contract is ridiculous and absurd [...] a draconian use of powers coupled with the recommendations in the bill which override fundamental civil rights of athletes, including the right against self-incrimination [...]. (Schwab, 2013)*

The fact that these fundamental human rights were threatened in the name of sport supports Wolf's statement on the limitations of sport's self-regulation: 'When private actors assume public functions, this does not unburden the state/world of states of their ultimate responsibility to mitigate the problems of legitimation associated with transnational private norm-setting and norm-enforcement.' The state could fulfill its responsibility, firstly, through 'external legitimation,' by integrating sport-related rules into the legal system and monitoring their enforcement to ensure no human rights or public interest objectives are threatened, and, secondly, through 'internal legitimation,' by helping these 'private actors' to address their own deficiencies (Wolf, 2014, pp. 301–302). However, proponents of sport exceptionalism have made it clear that they do not welcome these kinds of interventions.

A 2005 critique identified numerous inconsistencies in CAS's approach to doping allegations. Even though the practice of imposing penalties for doping offenses demonstrated that CAS treated them as criminal in nature, it failed to offer athletes the procedural protections, including the presumption of innocence and the right to appeal, that criminal cases require (Straubel, 2005, p. 1260). Moreover, in doping cases, CAS applied a higher standard of proof than the usual 'balance of probability' used in civil proceedings, whether or not the doping offense was criminal in nature (Oschutz, 2002, p. 696). Arbitrators use the principle of 'comfortable satisfaction' to decide cases: the 'standard of proof is greater than a mere balance of probability but less than proof beyond a reasonable doubt' (CAS 2015/A/3925). Similarly, as a 1998 CAS decision explained, when a 'high degree of satisfaction' has been established regarding a doping offence, the burden of proof shifts to the athlete, who may then raise the matter of intent to try to reduce the severity of the sanction (CAS 98/ 208). For a finding of NSF (no significant fault or negligence) or NF (no fault or negligence), the athlete has to demonstrate, on balance of probabilities, that the doping was not intentional (CAS 2015/A/4129). In a further attempt at deterrence, the IAAF Competition Rules of 2013/14 defined what it considers *aggravating circumstances*, including multiple doping violations, which warrant more severe sanctions and require the athlete to meet a higher burden of proof (IAAF, 2013/14, S. 40.6).

On the relatively minor role that *intent* plays in doping decisions, comments in one CAS decision revealed a more pragmatic rationale. To require proof of guilty intent, the arbitrators stated, 'would invite costly litigation that may well cripple federations – particularly those run on modest budgets – in their fight against doping' (CAS 94/129, S. 15). This concern for the financial wellbeing of sports federations stands in stark contrast to the earlier rationales for CAS, notably the claim that it was *athletes* who needed a less costly alternative to litigation for dispute resolution.

Straubel's recommendations provided practical steps to produce a system that was fairer and more predictable:

> *First, arbitrators [...] should have no current or recent connections with the governing bodies of the Olympic Movement or athletes that have been accused of doping violations. Second, the arbitrator selection process should do away with, or at the least minimize, the practice of parties appointing arbitrators. Third, the burden of proof used in doping cases should be more like that used in criminal cases. And, fourth, a mechanism, such as a single supervisory panel, should be created to reconcile conflicting precedent to ensure equal treatment and remove some of the arbitrariness of panel decisions (Straubel, 2005, p. 1272)*

Recommendations such as these, made more than a decade ago, have largely been ignored by CAS. With the exception of some minor revisions to the CAS Code, there have been few significant structural or procedural changes since 1993. As demonstrated above, several arbitrators had close connections with Olympic-related sports bodies, up to and including the IOC hierarchy, and there was evidence of role-switching between arbitrator and counsel at CAS hearings. For athletes appealing doping penalties, the implications are particularly serious.

3.7. WADA CODE: MORE EFFECTIVE, MORE INTRUSIVE

The WADA Code has undergone several revisions, most recently in 2007 and 2015, primarily for the purpose of strengthening its effectiveness through harsher penalties. On the issue of athletes' rights, two changes in the 2007 Code raised concerns among advocates and some sports lawyers: an increase in the suspension time for violations 'with aggravating circumstances' (for example, multiple offenses) from two years to four, and the introduction of a 'plea bargain.' Article 10.6 provided for the athlete to 'avoid the imposition of an increased sanction for aggravating circumstances by promptly admitting the anti-doping rule violation…' (quoted in Kauffman-Kohler and Rigozzi, 2007, p. 36.).

In a legal opinion solicited by WADA, Kaufmann-Kohler and Rigozzi (2007) examined whether Article 10.6 contravened the right to silence, the right not to incriminate oneself, and the presumption of innocence, as upheld by ECHR and the EC Convention. Noting that the WADA rule resembled a plea bargain, thereby raising 'the risk that any anti-doping organization may abuse process and threaten to charge an athlete… in order to obtain a decision,' they nevertheless concluded that CAS, and ultimately SFT, provided 'a sufficient safeguard' against unfairness (Kauffman-Kohler & Rigozzi, 2007, S. 112). Significantly, they emphasized that CAS, as a private adjudicator:

> *is not under a direct obligation to enforce*
> *international and national instruments of protection*

*of human rights. However, at least as a matter of
caution, it should apply the guarantees set out by
these instruments by way of analogy. Moreover [...]
[CAS is] required to enforce the athletes'
fundamental rights guaranteed by private law and
cannot ignore the relevant rules of competition law.
(Kauffman-Kohler & Rigozzi, 2007, S. 144)*

The force of this statement was somewhat diminished by
the authors' footnote which endorsed a previous legal opinion claiming that international support for the Code strongly
justified 'any infringement of the athlete's individual freedoms' (Kauffman-Kohler & Rigozzi, 2007, fn. 128).

Revisions developed in 2013 and introduced into the 2015
version of the WADA Code were in the areas of 'smarter'
evidence-gathering and prosecution; better testing and analysis;
harsher penalties for intentional dopers; more flexibility for
inadvertent dopers; and some procedural changes to promote
fairness. Rigozzi and his colleagues also assessed these revisions as part of a Swiss research project on the WADA Code.
They investigated the extent to which the changes produced a
'smarter, fairer and clearer Code,' concluding, unsurprisingly,
that 'each amendment that makes the fight against doping
more effective tends to make it more intrusive,' thereby raising
issues of 'privacy, data protection and scientific integrity of its
processes' (Rigozzi et al., 2013, p. 37). On one issue related to
athletes' rights, they pointed to the amendment allowing anti-
doping organizations to omit the Code's explanatory
'Comments' from their own rules, thereby implying that athletes were assumed to be knowledgeable about and in agreement with the content of those sections.

Although Rigozzi et al. applauded the Code's drafters for
their 'commitment [...] to voluntarily align the WADA Code
with the tenets of human rights law,' and the implied warning

to stakeholders that accused athletes' rights are 'paramount and should not be disregarded,' they pointed out that, overall, 'the references to human rights and the ECHR remain either purely aspirational or too vague...' (Rigozzi et al., 2013, p. 37).

While appearing to involve stakeholders throughout the revision process, WADA made several amendments to the 2015 Code after participants had approved the purported final draft at the November 2013 WADA conference in Johannesburg. In a follow-up commentary, Rigozzi et al. pointed out the procedural problems of adding significant last-minute amendments, most notably WADA's apparent disregard for good governance and the absence of accompanying documentation. On substantive issues, they noted that the amendments included a new concept of 'intentionality' and predicted that CAS panels might have difficulty reconciling it with traditional concepts of 'Fault or Negligence,' ultimately resulting in 'different lines of precedents detrimental to legal security' (Rigozzi, Viret, & Wisnosky, 2014, p. 4). There is little evidence that their commentary was heeded.

On the 'health risk' criterion, WADA's 2018 list of banned substances excluded alcohol 'after careful consideration,' but it recommended that IFs include rules to test and sanction offenders (WADA, 2018a, P1). Cannabinoids, first listed in 2005, remained on the list, primarily because of their illegality in many jurisdictions and alleged violation of 'the spirit of sport.' There had been ongoing debates about marijuana since the 1998 Rebagliati controversy (see Chapter 4), including, in 2013, the view that it had been added to WADA's list not because of performance-enhancing qualities, but because of perceived 'moral turpitude' (Dreier, 2013). Synthetic cannabidiol, a non-psychoactive compound used for pain relief, was removed from WADA's 2018 list.

3.8. SECOND CHANCES OR LIFE BANS?

Mainstream media are more than willing to circulate the myth that justice has been done as they provide details of doping allegations, defenses, decisions, and penalties, along with the rare redemption story to demonstrate a happy ending, a key ingredient being the athlete's reported remorse. Accounts of 'unrepentant' drug cheats rarely mention the fact that the strict liability principle imposed by CAS is a blunt instrument that, in the end, distinguishes only between innocence and guilt, ignoring intent or degrees of culpability. As a result, public opinion is not kind to accused athletes who, for good reasons, refuse to present themselves as guilty or remorseful.

In general, the principle of having 'served one's time' allows those found guilty of fraud, or even more serious offenses, to be rehabilitated and reintegrated into society. In 2004, a New Zealand boxer who had served a four-year prison term for the manslaughter of his infant daughter was selected for the Olympic team, apparently because of 'the general feeling of the New Zealand public.' A number of American and Australian men found guilty of armed robbery and drink driving were similarly permitted to compete in the Olympics (George, 2009, p. 52).

In one of the few cases involving a female athlete, American swimmer Tammy Crow, who was convicted of manslaughter following a fatal car accident, competed in the Athens 2004 Olympics (George, 2009, p. 52). Infamous, for different reasons, was American figure skater Tonya Harding, who competed at the Lillehammer 1994 Winter Olympics. Harding's ex-husband and bodyguard were behind an attack on rival Nancy Kerrigan a month before the Olympics. Harding subsequently pleaded guilty to the charge of hindering the investigation, and the US Figure Skating Union imposed a life ban, marking the end of her skating career.

In 2002–2003, two Australian male swim coaches accused of inappropriate sexual touching received more support from the media and the women's swimming community than the young women who were testifying against them. The 'everyone was doing it' defense justified full body massages, according to their argument (Lenskyj, 2013, pp. 91–93). One, Scott Volkers, was subsequently banned from working with children in Australia, but continued his coaching career with Brazil's national team in 2016 as well as working as a consultant coach in South Africa (Skinner, 2017). The other, Greg Hodge, successfully sued his accuser for defamation. In dramatic contrast, second chances are frequently withheld from athletes with doping histories, and 'everyone is doing it' is no defense – unless the athlete is Lance Armstrong. In November 2017, an American district judge allowed Armstrong to use evidence of widespread doping in professional cycling as a part of his defense in a civil fraud trial, but only in reference to the US Postal Service's sponsorship (Schrotenboer, 2017).

For track and field athletes accused of doping, the IAAF's definition of 'aggravating circumstances' names 'multiple violations' as a justification for the most severe sanctions. When African American sprinter Justin Gatlin won the 100 m race in London at the 2017 World Athletics Championships, his victory was met with booing and jeering from the crowd, many of whom wanted Jamaican Usain Bolt to win his last race before retiring. Most media inaccurately labeled Gatlin a 'two-time drug cheat' (Foster, 2017) who, to make matters worse, was allegedly 'unrepentant' (Cox, 2017). IAAF head Sebastian Coe expressed his displeasure at Gatlin's victory, thereby validating further public censure. Following more careful fact-checking of Gatlin's history, a *New York Times* reporter found only one proven doping violation, followed by a four-year ban, in 2006. The first alleged offence had involved amphetamines in a prescribed medication for attention deficit disorder, and Gatlin had successfully appealed the IAAF's two-year ban (Powell, 2017). A few years earlier, the media's fondness for freely applying the 'disgraced drug cheat' label had prompted Australian Olympic cyclist Mark French to sue a newspaper and a radio station for defamation. In 2005, CAS had upheld French's appeal and set aside the first CAS decision and the two-year doping sanction (CAS 2004/A/651).

In 2014, an English hurdler, Callum Priestley, retired at the age of 21 following a positive test for the performance-enhancing drug clenbuterol. The UK Anti-Doping Agency gave him a two-year suspension, while the British Olympic Association (BOA), as was their custom, banned him from the Olympics for life. As early as 2011, WADA had acknowledged that meat contaminated with clenbuterol was common in some countries, including China and Mexico, but since Priestley had been training in South Africa, where there was no evidence of a systemic problem, he would have to provide evidence of contaminated meat. In 2017, on the same day that German public television station ARD released a documentary and article titled Doping – Top Secret, WADA issued a statement regarding clenbuterol and the difficulties of determining pharmacological or meat contamination sources. It concluded that attempts at disciplinary measures against athletes who had low levels of clenbuterol and who had visited countries such as China or Mexico would probably not succeed, and 'would be very unfair to the athletes concerned' (WADA, 2017a). This outcome did not provide much comfort for Priestley.

Priestley, like several other male athletes in the UK, was subject to the BOA bylaw imposing lifetime bans for doping violations, a policy that was put in place in 1992. In 2011, after WADA challenged the BOA bylaw for its non-compliance with the Code, BOA appealed to CAS. As the CAS decision noted, 24 of the 25 British athletes who previously appealed the life-ban bylaw had been successful, and BOA, like all NOCs that sign on to the WADA Code, cannot impose an 'extra' or a 'double sanction' of this kind (CAS 2011/A/2658, S. 50) The CAS decision allowed UK sprinter Dwain Chambers and cyclist David Millar, both serving life bans, to compete in the London 2012 Olympics. Chambers' agent, Siza Agha, was highly critical of BOA's conduct during the CAS case, most notably its public statement that 'We have standards and the rest of the world doesn't.' Agha went on to identify the BOA's 'colonialist arrogance' that would not bode well for the UK's reputation in the lead-up to the London 2012 Olympics (quoted in Palmer, 2012).

A CAS decision issued in October 2011 had followed a similar rationale in overturning Rule 45 of the Olympic Charter banning athletes with doping suspensions of more than six months from competing in the next Olympics (CAS 2011/O/2422). The CAS panel, led by Richard McLaren, found this to be a violation of the principle of double jeopardy, arguing that Rule 45 was not 'a pure condition of eligibility' but rather a disciplinary sanction imposed in addition to the doping suspension. The panel distinguished between the IOC's eligibility criteria, which should be based solely on an athlete's performance, and WADA's sanctions, based on doping offenses. It ruled that the IOC regulation 'operates as, and has the effect of, a disciplinary sanction' (S. 43), thereby imposing two penalties for the same offence and violating the double jeopardy principle. It found that the rule was not in compliance with the WADA Code; it constituted 'a substantive change,' violated the IOC's own statutes, and was 'invalid and unenforceable' (S. 61).

The timing of these two appeals, in the lead-up to the London 2012 Summer Olympics, is noteworthy. Among the athletes who benefitted, an estimated 50 were in men's track and field and many were Black, including LaShawn Merritt and Dwain Chambers. Had CAS supported the IOC and BOA bans, the field of competitors would have been significantly diminished. Although their disqualification would have threatened the success of track events at London 2012, UK sports leaders, including Olympics Minister Hugh Robertson and IAAF president/London 2012 CEO Sebastian Coe, continued their vigorous defense of BOA's life ban (BOA get backing, 2012).

Rule 45 was removed from the Charter, but, four years later, changes to the 2015 WADA Code in effect reintroduced it, by increasing the two-year ban for doping offenses to four years (unless proven to be unintentional), so that disqualification from a future Olympic Games was automatic and inevitable.

3.9. ANTI-DOPING AGENCIES AND GOVERNANCE PROBLEMS

In light of the Olympic industry's virtually unfettered power over world sport, achieved in large part by the IOC's oversight of WADA and CAS, external critiques of these organizations' governance problems are unlikely to bring about change. In fact, WADA itself has complained of the IOC's excessive interventions and reluctance to withdraw its representatives from WADA's board and executive committee (Ford, 2017). It currently has six 'Olympic Movement' members, four of whom, including president Craig Reedie, are IOC members and six who are government sport officials. Other aspects of what critics have called 'inherent and demonstrated conflict of interest' include the IOC's and other sports bodies' funding of WADA's $28m annual budget, with the US Olympic Committee as the largest single contributor

(Bowen, Katz, Mitchell, Polden, & Walden, 2017, p. 129). If WADA were 'too successful' in detecting doping violations, the reputations of these SGBs would suffer.

In 2017, in a further development in the fight against doping, the IOC set up an 'independent not-for-profit Swiss foundation,' the Independent Testing Authority (ITA), for the purpose of conducting year-round drug-testing in all Olympic sports. Like other Olympic industry terminology, 'independent' appeared to have a special meaning in this context. Although ITA's executive committee has an 'independent chair' and an 'independent member,' it also has two IOC members and one IF representative. The Institute of National Anti-Doping Agencies (NADO) was among the many sports-related bodies to criticize this as yet another costly 'top-down global testing bureaucracy... that preserves a conflict of interest' through its close ties with the IOC. It was suggested that the IOC members of WADA had a vested interest in preserving the Olympic brand, and thus erred on the side of leniency in doping cases (Institute, 2017). By December, 2017, ITA had a new responsibility: to hear appeals by individual Russians seeking to compete in the 2018 PyeongChang Olympics as so-called neutral athletes, even though their official designation of 'Olympic Athlete from Russia' (OAR) left little doubt as to their provenance. An IOC-dominated committee, the OAR Implementation Group, determined which Russian athletes qualified in this category.

NADO was equally critical of another 2017 IOC initiative that removed all sanctioning power from anti-doping organizations, purportedly 'following the democratic principle of the 'separation of powers'' (IOC, 2017a). CAS would then be the sole body responsible for the sanctioning of individuals found doping and of organizations that WADA has declared non-compliant. NADO noted, as others had done, that the ICAS president, John Coates, was also an IOC

Vice-President, an arrangement that failed to suggest genuine 'separation of powers' (Institute, 2017, pp. 2–3).

Further objecting to this change, NADO claimed, 'in the majority of current cases, CAS is not needed because sanctioning decisions are sound' – excluding, they should have added, those of the non-compliant Russian anti-doping agency, RUSADA. Moreover, published CAS cases showed a number of athletes' challenges to sanctions imposed by national anti-doping agencies. The Jamaica Anti-Doping Commission (JADCO), for example, was respondent in eight appeals by six individual athletes between 2012 and 2014; three were upheld, two partially upheld, two dismissed and one lacking jurisdiction. Presumably, JADCO's decisions were not consistently sound.

3.10. FIVE WOMEN, FIVE CAS DOPING DECISIONS

It is not difficult to find inconsistencies in CAS doping decisions, as demonstrated by the outcomes in appeals launched by five women in the period 2014–2017. The appellants were a Kenyan athlete identified as F., Sherone Simpson, Maria Sharapova, Olga Abramova, and Therese Haug. On the specific issue of following bad advice from trusted advisers, Sharapova's and Johaug's experiences exemplify the negative consequences of doing so. At the same time, the differences between the two decisions on this issue led critics to point to CAS's chronic problems of unpredictability and inconsistency (Pielke, 2017, WADC, 2017a).

After Athletics Kenya suspended F., a female distance runner, for six months for a positive doping test, CAS partially upheld her appeal of 2015, reducing the ban to four months (CAS 2015/A/3899). She had purchased throat medication

believing that it contained no prohibited substance, as confirmed by the pharmacist. As the sole arbitrator noted, an
increase in doping cases in Kenya was not 'a factor that
weighs against the athlete' and the 'penalty imposed was to
some extent conditioned by those cases [...]' (S. 65). Finding
the six-month penalty to be too severe for the offence, the
decision stated, 'Indeed, IAAF Rule 40.8 seems to be an independent sanction not imposed on athletes under the WADC'
(S. 72). At the same time, it reiterated that it was the athlete's
responsibility 'to take proper precautions,' in this case by
consulting a doctor rather than a pharmacist (S. 64).

In somewhat similar circumstances in 2014, CAS had
reduced the sanction that JADCO had imposed on sprinter
Sherone Simpson from 18 months to six (CAS 2014/A/3572).
The panel found some negligence, but acknowledged that she
had done six hours of online research, and that 'no way short
of a lab test' would have identified the prohibited substance
in a supplement, but added: 'The Panel would wish this case
at least to serve as a further warning to all involved in sports
subject to the WADA code not to repose undue trust in
others' (S. 10.43). Paul Greene, Simpson's counsel and a specialist in the protection of athletes' rights, documented the
injustices that she and another Jamaican runner, Asafa
Powell, had suffered. In his 2017 article titled 'When Athletes
Are Wrongly Sanctioned under the World Anti-doping
Code,' Greene explained that at the time of the CAS hearing,
delayed when JADCO refused to agree to expedited proceedings, Simpson and Powell had already served a 12-month ban
and endured 'immeasurable emotional and financial distress
from the ordeal.' As he warned, the anti-doping system must
'understand and accept that athletes' rights are sacrosanct'
(Greene, 2017, p. 345).

Unlike most CAS cases, Sharapova's appeal attracted
international media attention. On January 26, 2016, a

doping test had found meldonium in Sharapova's sample. This substance had been added to WADA's 2016 prohibited list, in effect from January 1, and the International Tennis Federation (ITF) had imposed a two-year suspension. As stated during the CAS proceedings, for the past ten years, her doctor had prescribed Mildronate for health reasons. Her agent, a member of a leading global sports agency, had responsibility for managing all anti-doping matters, 'whereabouts' information, and therapeutic use exemptions, but he had failed to check the 2016 changes to the prohibited list. In her appeal to CAS, Sharapova requested a finding of NSF and a reduced suspension. The panel rejected the NSF argument, but, finding less than SF, reduced the sanction to 15 months. On the question of 'significant fault' and CAS jurisprudence, the Sharapova decision emphasized that although past doping cases 'offer guidance to a panel, all those cases are very "fact specific" and no doctrine of binding precedent applies' (CAS 2016/A/4643, S. 1).

The decision commented at length on Sharapova's character, stressing that the award 'was not about an athlete who cheated,' there was 'no question of intent,' and 'under no circumstances, therefore, can the Player be considered to be an 'intentional doper'', (CAS 2016/A/4643, S. 101). Furthermore, the panel was critical of WADA and ITF for failing to notify athletes of new prohibited substances, including their brand names.

In another meldonium-related case seven months later, CAS canceled a one-year suspension imposed by the International Biathlon Union on Ukrainian athlete Olga Abramova, finding that she bore no significant fault for the adverse finding. Since the meldonium ban only came into effect on January 1, 2016, the CAS decision pointed to the 'very specific circumstances' of the case, stating that Abramova 'could not reasonably have known' that the substance would be in her blood on January 10, when she was tested (TAS-CAS, 2017d). Interestingly, Sharapova's positive sample had been collected on January 26, but her fault was evaluated more harshly that Abramova's.

In large part as a result of media commentaries, public opinion was not particularly kind to Sharapova. A Google search for 'Sharapova' and 'remorse' in November 2017 produced countless media stories from around the globe, with the majority condemning her failure to apologize or to display any kind of remorse following her positive doping test and the suspension. Even one of the more balanced commentaries in a Singapore online news source emphasized her ambition, 'chilliness,' and lack of humility but urged readers to give her a second chance (Brijnath, 2017).

One of the very few articles that took a different view was a *USA Today* opinion piece titled 'What a racket: Nike suspends Sharapova, but has stuck with men who do worse.' Critical of Nike for dropping Sharapova's sponsorship, this journalist identified a clear double standard. He pointed to six male sports celebrities whose sponsors, including Nike, had overlooked convictions for doping, domestic violence, and criminal offenses: Lance Armstrong, Tiger Woods, Ray Rice, Kobe Bryant, Justin Gatlin, and Michael Vick (Grinspan, 2016).

The case of Therese Johaug, a Norwegian cross-country skier, had a markedly different outcome to Sharapova's. Although very successful in world championships and the Olympics, her achievements and her sport did not have the same level of international recognition as Sharapova's. Johaug had followed the team doctor's advice to treat sunburnt lips with a cream that, unknown to both her and her doctor, contained a banned anabolic agent. The Norwegian NOC suspended her for 13 months, a decision that the International Ski Federation appealed on the grounds that it should be extended to between 16 and 20 months. CAS agreed and increased the sanction to 18 months. The decision included strongly worded criticism of Johaug for failing to read the packaging and for trusting her doctor. Overall, it admonished her for her lack of oversight, stating that, as an experienced international athlete, 'she should have been very familiar with the rigorous standards expected of an athlete such as herself' (CAS 2017/A/5110).

Legal scholar Roger Pielke identified clear inconsistencies between the Sharapova and Johaug decisions on a number of key points: an athlete's responsibility to check products, delegation of that responsibility to professionals, trust in doctors, level of fault, and appropriate sanction. He also noted that the panel characterized each woman in markedly different ways, despite similarities in the allegations (Pielke, 2017). It seems possible that Sharapova's top-ranked status may have led the panel to allow her to delegate responsibility to her similarly top-ranked agent, a privilege not extended to Johaug. Alternatively, as the WADC team of sports lawyers – Rigozzi, Viret, and Wisnosky – suggested, the Johaug panel may have sought to 'close a loophole' that had been created in the Sharapova decision by asserting that an athlete cannot escape responsibility by blaming a third party and that he/she should always provide oversight. They pointed out that the 'No Significant Fault' finding in Sharapova's case, despite her failure to engage in oversight, may have conveyed the wrong message: that is, the idea that a 'delegation of responsibility' defense was worth trying (WADC, 2017b).

Further evidence of inconsistency may be seen by comparing the Johaug decision with that of F., the Kenyan athlete. When she relied on her pharmacist's advice, the CAS panel told her she should have consulted a doctor, but when Johaug entrusted her team doctor with monitoring her medication, she was told she should have checked the ingredients herself.

In their commentary on Johaug, the WADC team noted that the decision referred to 13 past awards, a useful exercise to promote consistency, but leading to 'a risk of developing concepts unfamiliar to athletes beyond those provided' in the WADA code. They concluded that 'justice was not entirely done... in part due to the fact that CAS panels, as individual arbitral tribunal, are inherently ill-suited for insuring uniformity of jurisprudence.' The current model, based on the WADA code, assumes 'some form of doping-relevant, reprehensible act' (WADC, 2017b) – in other words, the presumption of guilt, a logical consequence of the strict liability principle.

These critiques point to the underlying tension in CAS decisions regarding precedent: too much reliance on past cases produces outcomes such as the Johaug award where the athlete becomes, in the words of the WADC commentary, 'collateral damage of the system' (WADC, 2017b). On the other hand, decisions that fail to reference past awards contribute to CAS's reputation as inconsistent and non-transparent.

3.11. UNRESOLVED: CLAUDIA PECHSTEIN

The Pechstein case poses an ongoing challenge to CAS's so-called 'supreme court' status. In 2009, the International Skating Union banned Pechstein for two years following suspicious blood values. No prohibited substances had been identified, but a comparison with previous samples showed an allegedly 'abnormal' increase in red blood cells, which may indicate blood doping. Pechstein had the dubious distinction of being the first athlete to suffer the impact of longitudinal profiling, with WADA's 2009 introduction of the Athlete Biological Passport (ABP). The ABP was designed 'to monitor selected biological variables over time that indirectly reveal the effects of doping' rather than relying on finding the actual banned substances (WADA, 2017c). Apparently, changes that 'indirectly reveal the effects' of any other source are ignored; doping is the default position. As McArdle pointed out, WADA's 'legally problematic' use of longitudinal profiling and CAS's support of it 'do not sit easily with European law' (McArdle, 2011, pp. 51, 63).

Pechstein's appeal to CAS was dismissed on the grounds that 'illicit manipulation of her own blood […] [remained] the only reasonable alternative sources of such abnormal values' (CAS 2009/A/1912-1913). Since 2009, her two appeals to SFT and three appeals to German courts challenged the validity of forced arbitration, the reliability of WADA's blood tests, and CAS arbitrators' purported independence from sports organizations. She also argued that she suffered from blood anomalies that affected test results. SFT reaffirmed the CAS decisions, as did the Regional Court of Munich. The Higher Regional Court, however, agreed that, at the time of Pechstein's signing the arbitration agreement, the majority of CAS arbitrators were nominated by sports bodies, a practice that put their independence into question. Finally, in 2016, the German Federal Court of Justice dismissed her appeal. The CAS decision and its aftermath have been the subject of extensive critique and debate in legal circles, and there does not appear to be consensus on the case (see, for example, de Marco, 2016; Dickerson, 2015; Duval, 2016; Maisonneuve, 2016; Mavromati, 2016; McArdle, 2011, 2013). Some claimed that, despite its shortcomings, CAS is the best forum for sport disputes, while others argued that forced arbitration, longitudinal blood profiling, strict liability, limits on athletes' access to national courts, and other problems relating to the case, and to CAS in general, should be addressed. In the most recent development at the time of writing, the Federal

Constitutional Court of Germany had agreed to hear Pechstein's appeal.

3.12. THE RUSSIAN DOPING CONTROVERSY

In December 2014, German television station ARD aired yet another doping-related exposé, this one titled 'Top secret doping: How Russia makes its winners.' WADA began its investigations in 2015, and found sufficient reason to suspend the accreditation of the Moscow anti-doping laboratory. In May 2016, WADA commissioned CAS arbitrator Richard McLaren to investigate allegations of state-sponsored doping in Russia (see Hunter & Shannon, 2017). Two 'independent person reports' published in July and December, 2016 concluded that, in an 'institutional conspiracy' between 2011 and 2015, the Russian government and its sport-related infrastructure including the Moscow antidoping laboratory had protected Russian athletes: manipulation of test results and sample swapping allowed doping to go undetected. Further, the system of unofficial pre-competition 'washout' testing determined whether a newly-developed doping 'cocktail' with a very short detection window would show up during in-competition tests. The so-called 'Rodchenkov cocktail,' which comprised three drugs mixed with alcohol, was developed by the former laboratory head, later whistleblower, Dr Grigory Rodchenkov.

In July 2016, McLaren's findings concerning state-sponsored doping prompted the IOC to establish the Oswald Disciplinary Commission, a panel chaired by Swiss IOC member Denis Oswald, to conduct hearings involving 28 Russian athletes who were implicated in the report. As the IOC press release explained, the commission was set up because 'Prof. McLaren did not have the authority to bring forward Anti-Doping Rule Violation cases against individual athletes.' A panel comprising Oswald, Patrick Baumann, and Juan Antonio Samaranch (Junior) released its first decision on November 1, 2017, imposing a lifetime ban on Olympic competition on skiers Alexander Legkov and Evgeniy Belov, as well as erasure of their records and other related penalties (IOC sanctions, 2017b).

3.12.1. IAAF vs Anna Pyatykh and RUSAF

A CAS decision in October 2017 had already sent a clear message to any Russian athlete planning an appeal. The Anna Pyatykh case was characterized by the mainstream media as the first in a potential cascade of successful charges against individual Russians, based solely on the findings of the McLaren reports. The case involved the IAAF as appellant and the Russian Athletics Federation (RUSAF) and triple jumper Anna Pyatykh as respondents (CAS/2017/O/5039). At that time, RUSAF had been suspended pending investigations of state-sponsored doping, and therefore had been unable to conduct Pyatykh's hearing. The sole arbitrator was a relatively new CAS appointee, Jens Evald, and the invisible presence at the hearing was 'Independent Person' (IP) Richard McLaren, specifically identified in the IAAF's submission as 'a very reputable CAS arbitrator' (S. 56).

On the first doping charge, Pyatykh's sample, taken in 2007 and retested in 2017, had revealed a prohibited anabolic steroid. She explained that, as far as she could remember, it was an ingredient in a dietary supplement. A second and more serious charge, which she also denied, involved her alleged participation in the so-called 'washout schedule' of unofficial testing set up in Moscow's anti-doping laboratory. Although the 2013 document, referred to in the decision as the Excel Washout Schedule, gave only code numbers for athletes, McLaren had identified Pyatykh to the IAAF as one of the athletes in the washout testing program.

In his rationale for using the McLaren report, the sole arbitrator noted that different types of evidence can be used in an individual doping case. The Second Independent Person Report, following WADA's rules, allowed a case against an athlete to be established by 'any reliable means,' specifically, in this instance, three methods: contextual evidence, the Moscow Laboratory's testing procedures, and forensic evidence concerning sample manipulation (S. 89). This assembly of facts, Evald stated, is 'circumstantial evidence that can be used to establish' an anti-doping rule violation, referring to four other CAS awards that supported this finding (S. 91). In determining the four-year suspension, he found 'almost all aggravating factors' in the IAAF rules to be present: the violation was committed as part of a doping plan, and multiple prohibited substances were used on multiple occasions (S. 119).

Regardless of her innocence or guilt, Pyatykh's experience before CAS raises a number of questions and concerns, particularly in relation to the 'stacked decks' problem. RUSAF's failure to participate, although invited to do so, gave the impression that they had little interest in supporting or defending her (although admittedly their presence may have been a mixed blessing). This left an individual, relatively low-profile female athlete – successful in European competition but not in the Olympics – who was attempting to defend her actions of ten years earlier, in the context of the highly politicized Russian doping controversy. The poorly expressed English in her written submissions suggests that Pyatykh lacked the services of a competent interpreter during the preparation of her statements. She participated in the hearing via Skype, with the help of an interpreter, but there is no mention of counsel representing her. In contrast, the IAAF was more than adequately represented by four Kellerhals Carrard counsel, including veterans Ross Wenzel and Nicolas Zhinden. In short, this appeared to be a perfect test case to support the use of McLaren's findings as 'reliable' grounds for future sanctions against Russian athletes. As events unfolded in 2017, however, the IOC attempted to avoid any further individual appeals by invoking McLaren's reports and Rodchenkov's testimony to support the blanket disqualification of the Russian team from the 2018 PyeongChang Winter Olympics and the suspension of the Russian Olympic Committee.

3.12.2. CAS vs Oswald

By December 2017, the Oswald Commission had suffered the first challenge to its credibility. The Doping Hearing Panel of the International Bobsleigh and Skeleton Federation (IBSF) decided not to suspend seven Russian athletes, on the grounds that Rodchenkov's evidence had only been heard before McLaren, not before a proper hearing panel. The IBSF Doping Hearing Panel claimed that this was incompatible with international law, Swiss procedural law, and the EC Convention for the Protection of Human Rights regarding fair process (ISBF, 2017). IBSF itself then appealed to CAS, seeking to impose the suspensions, but, in January 2018, CAS announced that it did not have jurisdiction on the matter (TAS-CAS, 2018a).

In January 2018, 42 Russian athletes who had been disqualified from the 2018 PyeongChang Winter Olympics by the IOC's blanket life ban appealed to CAS. Based on the evidence, which included testimony by McLaren and Rodchenkov, the CAS decision of February 1 upheld 28 of the Russians' appeals, thereby making them eligible to compete in PyeongChang and reinstating their individual results from the 2014 Sochi Olympics. CAS partially upheld 11 appeals; the panel agreed that the evidence confirmed these athletes' anti-doping violations and disqualified them from the 2018 Olympics, but annulled the IOC's lifetime ban (TAS-CAS, 2018c). (The remaining three hearings were postponed.)

Although CAS's media release noted that the panels were dealing only with individual cases, and not with the question of a state-sponsored doping scheme, the fact that most appeals were upheld was hardly a ringing endorsement of the Oswald Commission or the McLaren reports. Because of the large number of awards, the reasoned decisions were not publicly available until several weeks later.

Predictably, the IOC and WADA expressed 'disappointment' and 'concern' at the decision, while trying to make the best of it by noting their 'satisfaction' regarding the guilty findings in 11 cases, and emphasizing that the 28 athletes had not been declared 'innocent' (IOC, 2018a, WADA, 2018b). In the same 'disappointed' vein, IOC president Bach claimed that the CAS decision showed 'the urgent need for reforms in the internal structure of CAS' (quoted in Kim, 2018). ICAS president and IOC member John Coates' statement of February 5 clearly revealed the dilemma facing both CAS and the IOC. Since 1993, both sides had been working on the problem of CAS's alleged dependence on the IOC, and this CAS decision could be seen as providing unprecedented evidence of CAS's independence. Yet Coates, as IOC member, had to acknowledge Bach's concerns, issuing assurances that 'CAS will continue to evolve to ensure consistency and quality of jurisprudence' (TAS-CAS, 2018d). In light of the limited 'evolution' of this tribunal since 1993, structural changes seem highly unlikely.

The final decision to invite any athlete to the Olympics is in the hands of the IOC executive, and predictably, it only took a few days for the IOC to reject the Russian Olympic committee's request to allow 15 of the Russian athletes and coaches to participate in the 2018 Olympics. Among the reasons given by the panel that assessed 'neutral' athletes was a passing reference to 'additional elements and/or evidence,' including data from the Moscow doping laboratory database and 'confidential information' from WADA that had not been available to the Oswald Commission (IOC, 2018b). In other words, when the IOC wants to shift the goalposts on issues of admissible evidence and due process, it has the power to do so.

In a somewhat unexpected move, Bach announced that the IOC would consider appealing the CAS decision to the SFT, a move that WADA supported (WADA, 2018b). The irony is remarkable: that the most powerful global sports organization would contemplate appealing to the 'court of last resort' for justice. Bach qualified the statement by noting that the IOC needed to examine the full reasoned decision before taking this step. As events unfolded, it seemed unlikely that the IOC would take this step.

Through its February 1, 2018, media release, the IOC complained that CAS had imposed a 'higher threshold on the necessary level of evidence than the Oswald Commission and former CAS decisions' (IOC, 2018a). Although in one of its early decisions (re Aleksandr Tretiakov), the Oswald Commission had referred to the WADA Code as its guide to 'Standards and Burden of Proof,' the same panel argued that the McLaren findings were serious enough to justify establishing 'a presumption that all top-level Russian athletes had been part of the [doping] system [...]' (IOC, 2017d, S. 88) – a statement that implied the presumption of guilt based on circumstantial evidence. In other words, it appears that the Oswald Commission itself had strayed from the 'comfortable satisfaction' standard. On the question of precedent, in an arbitration system that ostensibly does not rely on past decisions, this critique was irrelevant. Not having seen the reasoned decision, Oswald, Bach, and other IOC members nevertheless accused CAS of applying a 'criminal standard of proof,' an inference they made based on the CAS media release, which had merely stated that there was 'insufficient evidence' to support disqualifying the 32 Russians. A very public feud developed as the IOC held its annual meeting in the lead-up to the PyeongChang opening ceremony, with Bach and Richard Pound leading the attack on CAS and Coates, and charging that these developments were sabotaging the war on doping. Some more cynical commentaries on social media suggested that all of these key actors were playing out roles to redirect attention from the numerous inconsistencies arising from these cases.

On February 6, 2018, 45 Russian athletes and two coaches filed appeals with the AHD in PyeongChang, on the grounds that the IOC's refusal to invite them to participate was arbitrary and discriminatory, thereby constituting a sanction for an unproven doping offence, and that the selection process lacked transparency. AHD dismissed the appeals, stating that the selection process was an eligibility decision, and not a sanction. Unsurprisingly, the IOC, this time on the winning side, 'welcomed the decision.' The AHD panel avoided addressing the fact that four other CAS arbitrators (a three-member panel and a sole arbitrator) had cleared many of the same individual athletes a week earlier. The decision included a reference to the work of the IOC selection committee and the OAR Implementation Group, noting that time constraints and the large number of appeals meant that 'the process may not have been a perfect one' (CAS OG 18/02, 03, S. 7.15). These entire proceedings reveal yet again the unpredictability and unfairness of doping-related CAS decisions.

3.13. CONCLUSION

Global acceptance that the ends justify the means in the war against doping signifies another success for the proponents of sport exceptionalism. Rhetoric invoking the sanctity of 'clean sport' and 'level playing fields' serves to conceal several inconvenient truths, including low detection rates, intrusive surveillance, inconsistent CAS decisions, and internal governance disputes. Overall, the strict liability principle, characterized as harsh but essential, leaves athletes, particularly women and ethnic minorities, stripped of basic human rights protections. In this climate, the exposure of Russia's state-sponsored doping gave WADA and the IOC a high-profile victory on the anti-doping front, while the compromise solution allowing 169 Russian athletes to participate in the 2018 PyeongChang Olympics as so-called 'neutrals' gave the impression of 'fairness' and ensured that the field of competitors was not seriously diminished. However, none of the key players emerged unscathed from the Russian controversy, as numerous voices from within the Olympic industry expressed concerns that the 'chaotic' situation posed a threat to the anti-doping campaign. Whether the various calls for reform will result in systemic change within WADA, IOC, or CAS is a question yet to be resolved.

CHAPTER 4

DOPING, GENES, AND GENDER

While doping dominates the attention of CAS panels and the general public, important issues of gender and 'race'/ethnicity are also played out in two other related areas, identified in CAS jurisprudence as eligibility and discipline. The following discussion continues to investigate doping, with a focus on testosterone-related controversies and their impacts on gender-variant women and on racialized men. Finally, the experiences of female and male athletes charged with bringing themselves and/or their sport into 'disrepute' will be examined.

4.1. GENDER POLICING

It is axiomatic in sport circles that a 'level playing field' requires competitors to be divided into two strict categories: male and female. Equestrian sports are the only Olympic events in which men and women compete against each other. Concepts of gender fluidity and gender variance, widely accepted in social and legal contexts outside of sport, are for the most part rejected in high performance sport. All men are faster and stronger than all women, according to the binary thinking that characterizes most sport policy, so it would be unfair to pit the sexes against one another. As in the war against doping, the mainstream media support the majority view that 'fairness' demands draconian measures, and journalists can readily find 'real women' to complain about unfair competition and invoke 'level playing field' arguments to support the demonization of gender-variant women. It is in this context that female athletes with high levels of naturally occurring testosterone (hyperandrogenism), and transgender women who have transitioned from male to female struggle for justice.

The stigmatization, harassment and violence that gender-variant athletes have experienced are serious concerns. Many scholarly analyses of these issues present convincing arguments that the IAAF's and IOC's policies constitute gender policing: a twenty-first-century version of the invasive and humiliating sex tests, starting with 'nude parades,' to which all female athletes were subject from the 1960s to 1999. Anti-doping procedures introduced in the 1990s require that a urine sample be produced under direct observation, with the area of the athlete's body from nipple to knee exposed, a procedure that women, in particular, often find degrading and distressing (Mazanov, 2016, p. 177). No longer is the goal to prevent male athletes from masquerading as women, since the anti-doping observer who supervises the production of the urine sample will presumably recognize the difference. Rather, it is to establish whether a female athlete is 'woman enough' (Ferguson-Smith & Bavington, 2014; Genel et al., 2016; Schultz, 2012).

The moral crusade against gender-variant female athletes parallels the general tone of the war against doping: that is, it's a fight that must be won at all costs. Like rationales for harsh anti-doping measures and penalties, much of the rhetoric about unfairness to 'normal' female athletes conveys the message that a few gender-variant women may have to suffer for the greater good. That one woman, Indian runner Santhi Soundararajan, attempted suicide after details of her failed 'sex test' were leaked to the media was not sufficient, it seems, to raise awareness of the human cost of these practices.

4.2. THE T WORD: TESTOSTERONE

A discussion of controversies over hyperandrogenism necessarily begins by examining the assumption that testosterone defines maleness and determines athletic prowess. As a result of widespread acceptance of this flawed reasoning, testosterone levels are at the core of most eligibility issues. Contrary to the stereotypical labeling of testosterone as the 'male hormone' and estrogen as 'the female hormone,' these hormones are produced in both male and female bodies, but usually in different proportions.

Recent research shows that sex-related differences in testosterone are lower among athletes than non-athletes, and that there is complete overlap between the sexes (Healy et al., 2014). These findings should not come as a surprise to sport scientists. Exercise physiology research dating back to the 1980s showed that athletes differed from the non-athlete population on a number of measures, and, within the same sport, differences in body size and composition accounted for most sex differences. In terms of cardiovascular fitness, male and female athletes in the same sport shared more similarities with one other than with their sedentary, sex-matched counterparts (Drinkwater, 1984; O'Toole & Douglas, 1988).

Although countless other doping products have emerged in the last few decades, anabolic steroids, which are synthetic derivatives of testosterone, continue to account for almost half the number of doping violations documented by WADA. Suspicious samples are retested using the more advanced and costlier carbon isotope ratio test. In fact, there seems to be no end in sight to the ever-escalating costs of testing and retesting blood and urine samples in what might aptly be called the anti-doping industry.

Testosterone tests analyze the ratio of testosterone to epitestosterone (T/E ratio) in athletes' urine, in order to determine whether the testosterone is endogenous (produced naturally in the body) or exogenous (artificial). In 1983, the IOC established that T/E ratios above 6.1 should be treated as suspicious, but, in 2005, WADA lowered that ratio to 4.1, based in part on findings that Asian males tended to have lower T/E ratios than Caucasians. WADA's (2004) Technical Document on endogenous steroids directed laboratories to heed the 'significant variation between individuals' by adapting testing procedures accordingly: male or female, Asian or Caucasian (WADA, 2004, p. 2).

4.3. HYPERANDROGENISM

Several recent eligibility controversies involved female athletes with higher than average endogenous testosterone, a condition termed hyperandrogenism. Within that group are two subtypes: those whose bodies can use the testosterone and therefore are assumed to have an unfair advantage, and those who have androgen insensitivity syndrome (AIS) and do not benefit from testosterone. Regardless of anatomical, hormonal, and physiological variations evident at or before maturity, most individuals with hyperandrogenism identify as female.

Hyperandrogenism is associated with polycystic ovary syndrome (PCOS), a condition caused by naturally occurring elevated levels of androgens. PCOS may result in amenorrhea (a menstrual disorder), hirsutism and increased muscle bulk, and some studies have shown a greater incidence of PCOS among female athletes, in particular those in power sports, than among the general female population. Amenorrhea in athletes was a condition formerly assumed to be one of the three health problems that comprised the 'female athlete triad,' together with decreased bone mineral density and low energy availability (with or without eating disorders). Based on a study of 90 Swedish Olympic athletes, researchers at the Karolinska Institute found that PCOS, and not strenuous exercise, was the most common cause of menstrual disorders, and that none of these women had bone density problems. In a rare example of findings presented in a positive light, these researchers concluded that 'female athletes can perform exceedingly well at an elite level without endangering their health' (Hagmar et al., 2009, 1247; see also Rickenlund et al., 2003).

Most research on hyperandrogenism risks pathologizing yet another aspect of female physiology and legitimizing what may prove to be unnecessary medical interventions. For example, the authors of a 2011 study of PCOS and menstrual disorders in 18 adolescent swimmers suggested that hyperandrogenism may have preceded their intensive training, 'predisposed the choice of sport... [and] attenuated the clinical expression of their hyperandrogenism' (Coste et al., 2011). It appears, then, that these girls' physical abilities led them to choose activities that used and enhanced those strengths. Surely this is true of the vast majority of successful young athletes: their body types and physical abilities lead them to certain sports, intense training enhances their abilities, and they are successful and motivated to pursue these sports. Young male athletes who fit this profile would be applauded, rather than subjected to the 'clinical, biologic, and ultrasonic investigations' that these researchers conducted (Coste et al., 2011).

Recent research on hyperandrogenism, testosterone, and related issues is dominated by two groups of researchers, one headed by Dr Stéphane, Bermon, Monaco Institute of Sports Medicine and Surgery, and the other by Dr Peter Sonksen, University of Southampton, UK. Several members of Bermon's team had or continue to have overlapping, and potentially conflicting roles in the IOC, IAAF and WADA as members of various medical commissions and advisory groups. These include Bermon, who is a member of the IAAF and IOC working groups on hyperandrogenic female athletes and transgender athletes, and Pierre-Yves Garnier, the director of the IAAF Health and Science Department. The team also included a number of researchers affiliated with the Karolinska Institute, Stockholm, the most prominent being Swedish IOC member Arne Ljunqvist, who had also served as a member of the IAAF Medical Committee and the WADA Executive. Regardless of their excellent credentials and reputations, the insider status of several key researchers in this area should be recognized. While their publications name WADA, IAAF, and national anti-doping agencies as funding sources, they do not consistently acknowledge the potential for conflict of interest when serving as 'in-house' researchers for the same organizations that are conducting gender policing.

In 1996, Sonksen's team had initiated the GH-2000 project. involving a multi-national research group funded by the EU and the IOC for the purpose of developing a reliable methodology to detect growth hormone (GH) misuse in professional sport. Following its final report in 1999, the IOC and WADA requested further validation of the methodology, and the GH-2004 project, funded by the US Anti-Doping Agency and WADA and led by Sonksen, was set up at the

University of Southampton (Growth Hormone 2004 Study, 2017). Like Bermon's team, these researchers had an extensive dataset on which to base specific statistical analyses that would contribute to understanding testosterone levels and hyperandrogenism.

The hyperandrogenism controversies began in 2009 with the IAAF's mishandling of a situation involving a 19-year-old South African sprinter, Caster Semenya. Following her success in the World Championships and subsequent accusations from rival teams that she was not 'a real woman,' she was subjected to months of unspecified medical interventions before being allowed to compete again. Details of her so-called intersex or hermaphroditic condition, also known as Disorders of Sexual Development (DSD), were widely publicized in the global media. Although some other female athletes had experienced similar mistreatment, none had been exposed to that level of international media scrutiny and humiliation, and Semenya's case has been the subject of extensive critique (Henne, 2015; Lenskyj, 2013, Ch. 6; Schultz, 2012). Clearly, from the IAAF point of view, a repeat of this public relations' debacle should be avoided. More importantly, from a social justice perspective, there was widespread international concern that the rights and privacy of this young woman had been violated.

In 2011, after 18 months of 'expert' review, the IAAF announced its *Regulations Governing Eligibility of Females with Hyperandrogenism to Compete in Women's Competition* (IAAF, 2011). The document began by stating that sex difference in performance 'is known to be predominantly due to higher levels of androgenic hormones in males resulting in increased strength and muscle development.' It then invoked a mixture of health and ethical principles including 'a respect for the fundamental notion of fairness of competition in female athletics' and 'a respect for the very essence of the male and female classifications in Athletics' (IAAF, 2011, p. 1). Regardless of the rhetoric, these classifications are socially constructed. There is no *essence*, nor is there a clear male/female binary; scientists have identified at least six markers of sex, none of which are binary. The new regulations emphasized the need for confidentiality throughout the medical process, and concluded by acknowledging that 'females with hyperandrogenism may compete in women's competition in Athletics subject to compliance with IAAF Rules and Regulations' (2011, p. 1). At that time, IAAF had not defined the level of testosterone considered acceptable in order to qualify for women's competition, and the authorities operated on a case-by-case basis.

4.3.1. A 'Retrospective Clinical Study' and Its Victims

In the IAAF's campaign to detect hyperandrogenism, 'suspicion-based testing,' as Schultz (2012, p. 449) aptly termed it, had serious consequences for many young athletes, most of whom were racialized women from non-western countries. Following complaints at the London 2012 Olympics, the IAAF began investigating four female athletes aged 18–21, all from rural areas of developing countries. Rather than give up their athletic careers, but aware that their performance levels would probably be affected, the young women agreed to have surgery to remove internal testes that accounted for their high testosterone levels. The medical team also 'proposed' additional surgery unrelated to athletic performance – 'femininizing vaginoplasty' and partial clitoridectomy – along with estrogen replacement therapy. These procedures were conducted at a French hospital that collaborates with the IAAF to treat athletes with so-called disorders of sexual development. The specialists involved in this process, together with other medical researchers, published a retrospective clinical study (Fenichel et al., 2013), the goal of which was to determine whether high levels of testosterone in the four young women would reveal 'undiagnosed XY DSD' – that is, a chromosomal disorder of sexual development. Bermon was one of the co-authors, although his association with the IOC and the IAAF was not disclosed in this article.

In a strongly-worded critique of the entire procedure, Sonksen et al. (2015b) identified serious ethical problems: '[...] the removal of gonads and the clitoral mutilation for the purposes of eligibility in the women's category is unethical [...] [and] The additional feminizing procedures are particularly alarming' (Sonksen et al., 2015b, p. 826). The publication of these women's confidential medical records and other personal information contravened both medical ethics and the IAAF Regulations of 2011. Personal information provided by Fenichel et al. was sufficiently detailed to allow their actual identities to be deduced. As well, Sonksen et al. noted, the authors failed to provide evidence that ethical approval for the study had been granted.

Other aspects of this unethical episode demand critique. These young women were hospitalized in a foreign country, away from their usual support systems. From the report, it appears that their health knowledge was not extensive; they seemed unaware that they had what western doctors considered a medical problem, and asked questions about menstruation, sexual activity and childbearing. The stark clinical language of the report came dangerously close to portraying these vulnerable young women as freaks – 'male bone morphotype, no breast development' – rather than gender variant females. In short, they were treated as human guinea pigs, a 'convenience sample' that would yield interesting data to support the continued disqualification of genetically gifted women. As many critics have pointed out, the genetic gifts enjoyed by the Usain Bolts of the running world are admired, while these women's talents are pathologized.

Racism is at work in all of these controversies, and many western sportswomen enjoy an advantage: they understand the rules of engagement and can take the necessary steps to appear conventionally 'feminine' if they choose to do so. Among top female sprinters and middle- and long-distance runners, Black or white, from western countries, there are unlikely to be many full-breasted, wide-hipped women, since a specific body type is key to success in these events. It is not a coincidence that muscular, flat-chested runners from western countries have escaped the level of media and public scrutiny aimed at their African and South Asian counterparts.

4.3.2. Dutee Chand

In 2014, the Athletics Federation of India and the Sports Authority of India banned 18-year-old Indian sprinter Dutee Chand from competing in women's events, on the grounds that she failed to meet the IAAF's eligibility requirements. These organizations had authorized a number of invasive medical examinations aimed at determining that Chand had hyperandrogenism.

Chand appealed to CAS (CAS, 2014/A/3759), naming as respondents the Athletic Federation of India and the IAAF. Among expert witnesses for the IAAF were Bermon, Ritzen and Ljungqvist. The panel noted that, in view of these men's involvement in preparing and implementing the regulations, their independence and impartiality could be questioned, but concluded that they were acting 'as independent professional experts.' Supporting Chand as expert witnesses were Sonksen and his colleague Richard Holt, Katrina Karkazis, a cultural anthropologist, and Sari van Anders, a psychologist specializing in social neuroendocrinology.

Paula Radcliffe, MBE (as identified in the CAS decision) served as a witness for the IAAF. Acknowledging that she was not a scientist and was basing her position on existing scientific studies, she nevertheless claimed that her own experience 'of growing up and competing as a female athlete' (S. 339) – or more precisely, as a non-hyperandrogenic female athlete – reinforced what experts were saying about the testosterone advantage, when compared to 'natural talent and dedication' (S. 337). Her statement implied that athletes with hyperandrogenism exploited their 'unnatural' talent and did not need to work as hard as 'normal' women, thereby posing a threat to 'the level playing field.'

Much of the 161-page Chand decision comprised a scientific debate between the Bermon team and the Sonksen team. It is interesting to note that, when discussing the IAAF's previous investigations of hyperandrogenism, Bermon referred to the four subjects of the much-criticized 2013 retrospective clinical study report that he had co-authored (Fenichel et al., 2013). However, the exact number of women and other details were redacted in the published version of the CAS decision, presumably as a result of the criticism the original article had received. Details of Chand's medical history were also redacted.

The CAS panel that heard Chand's appeal was headed by relatively new arbitrator Annabelle Bennett, and included Richard McLaren. First appointed in 2014, Bennett served on AHDs at the 2014 Sochi Olympics and 2016 Rio Olympics. There are no specific references to sport in her profile according to information on the CAS website and elsewhere, but, in addition to a long list of achievements in law as barrister and judge, she has a significant science and health-related background, including a PhD in biochemistry, and has served on numerous committees, boards and task forces related to science, health and medicine.

The CAS panel agreed with the broader scientific community that 'there is no single determinant of sex' (CAS, 2014/A/ 3759, S. 35.c), thereby challenging traditional biology-based definitions and binary thinking. The decision confirmed that the IAAF regulations were discriminatory, and, therefore, the IAAF bore the burden of proof to establish that they were 'necessary, reasonable and proportionate' to establish 'a level playing field' (S. 450). The panel partially upheld Chand's appeal, suspended IAAF's hyperandrogenism regulations for two years, and required, within that time, that the IAAF submit 'written evidence and expert reports' to support its claim that athletes like Chand had a performance advantage. Specifically, it called for expert evidence of 'the actual degree of athletic performance advantage' resulting from hyperandrogenism (CAS, 2014/A/3759, p. 160). In July 2017, at IAAF's request, CAS extended the two-year deadline by two months, and in January 2018, CAS announced that proceedings would be suspended for another six months, during which the IAAF Hyperandrogenism Regulation would remain suspended (TAS-CAS, 2018b) – a possible reprieve for Chand but, at the time of writing, a continuing unresolved issue.

4.4. QUANTIFYING THE UNQUANTIFIABLE

It seems fair to assume that the actual degree of advantage for women with hyperandrogenism is impossible to measure, but a number of researchers, most notably those with long associations with the IAAF and IOC, took up the challenge. On July 3, 2017, a month before the two-year deadline, the IAAF issued a press release titled 'Levelling the Playing Field in Female Sport: New Research Published in the British

Journal of Sports Medicine' (*BJSM*). The authors, unsurprisingly, were members of the Bermon team. Summarizing the findings, it stated, 'Among other things, the study found that in certain events female athletes with high testosterone levels benefit from a 1.8% to 4.5% competitive advantage over females with lower testosterone levels.' As quoted in the press release, Bermon added to its high moral tone by stating that the researchers' goal was 'to defend, protect and promote fair female competition.' '[I]magine the magnitude of the advantage for female athletes with testosterone levels in the normal male range,' he warned, if they were allowed to compete against so-called normal women (IAAF, 2017).

The co-authored report published in *BJSM* presented the findings in a more nuanced and cautious manner than the IAAF's press release. The subjects were 2127 male and female athletes who had competed in the 2011 IAAF World Championships in Daegu, Korea, and the 2013 championships in Moscow, and whose blood samples were tested for serum androgen concentrations (testosterone) (Bermon & Garnier, 2017). This study was part of a bigger research project on serum androgen, funded mainly by the IAAF and WADA, with earlier published reports including Robinson et al. (2012) and Bermon et al. (2014).

The 2012 article by Robinson et al. had focused on methodology, noting that mandatory pre-competition blood testing, first introduced in the 2011 IAAF event, was intended 'to give a clear signal to the world athletic community' concerning the 'smart implementation' of the Athlete Biological Passport (ABP) in the 'fight against doping' (Robinson et al., 2012, p. 149). Bermon et al.'s 2014 article reported on findings from 849 female athletes, with the objective of measuring serum androgen levels prior to implementing the blood steroidal module of the ABP. The WADA/IAAF research team (Bermon, Robinson, Garnier et al.) played an important role in developing the ABP, as well as having at hand an appropriate and convenient dataset for further statistical analysis. Since the study that examined the so-called 'testosterone advantage' was not published until 2017, it seems likely that Bennett's instructions to the IAAF precipitated this particular focus in their analysis of the 2011 data.

In fact, the results failed to provide clear evidence of the 'testosterone advantage.' There were only five out of 21 track and field events in which women in the high testosterone group experienced a competitive advantage: the 400 m, 400 m hurdles, 800 m, hammer throw, and pole vault. Female athletes in 16 events, including 100 m and 200 m sprints and most middle- and long-distance runs – that is, about three-quarters of the track and field program – did not fit this pattern. Findings involving male athletes were also of interest: hammer throwers had lower testosterone levels than other males in track and field, while male sprinters showed higher values. The authors cautioned that the study design 'cannot provide evidence for causality between androgen levels and athletic performance, but can indicate *associations* […]' (Bermon & Garnier, 2017, p. 1312, emphasis added), a crucial distinction that the IAAF press release appears to have ignored.

In a separate review of the research, Bermon (2017) stated that females with high androgen levels had '2–5% competitive advantage,' rounding up the 1.8–4.5% finding reported by Bermon and Garnier (2017). Overall, Bermon concluded: 'In females, androgens increase lean body mass, oxygen-carrying capacity, visuospatial abilities, and aggressivity, which are decisive factors of sport performance' (Bermon, 2017, p. 1).

This sweeping statement demands further analysis. For example, the research showed that gymnastics and orienteering were the main sports in which superior visuospatial ability was a benefit, and it was not clear how high-androgen female athletes in other sports enjoyed this reported advantage. Furthermore, Bermon claimed that 'aggressive behaviour and risk taking' were 'important determinants of sports performance,' an assumption that overlooked equally important social/cultural determinants of competitiveness, ambition, drive, and other psychological traits. Overall, his summary invoked the long-standing and widely challenged stereotype of the female athlete as a deficient male: weaker, more timid, less competitive, lacking 'the right stuff' (testosterone) to match her stronger, tougher, more aggressive male counterpart. Certainly, differences have been found on many of these physiological and psychological measures, but sports scientists should not ignore the existence of significant similarities between male and female athletes, and the significant differences between the athlete and non-athlete populations.

In a debate played out in the pages of the *Journal of Clinical Endocrinology & Metabolism* since 2014, Healy, Sonksen et al. reported on the endocrine profiles of 813 male and female elite athletes. Their analysis revealed that women's lean body mass was 85% of men's, a difference that they considered 'sufficient to account for sex differences in performance,' thereby challenging the IOC's and the IAAF's single-minded reliance on the testosterone argument (Healy et al., 2014, p. 294). On the question of gender-based differences in testosterone levels, their analysis found 'complete overlap of the range of concentration seen' (p. 303). Members of the other team, Ritzen, Ljungqvist, Garnier, Bermon, and others, challenged those findings in a letter to the editor (Ritzen et al., 2015, p. 307). Included in their critiques was the claim that testing under resting conditions, as Healy et al. had done, produced different results, that they had not ruled out hyperandrogenism or androgen insensitivity syndrome, and that testosterone may have accounted for sex-related differences in lean body mass. Sonksen and his colleagues convincingly rebutted all of these arguments, concluding by stating that the 2013 Bermon et al. publication, cited by Ritzen et al., actually supported rather than disputed their findings (Sonksen et al., 2015a). These are important debates among experts in the field, a fact that the IAAF has consistently failed to acknowledge.

On the Chand case, CAS's January 2018 press release noted that IAAF had filed 'expert reports and legal submissions,' including 'draft revised regulations that would only apply to female track events […] between 400 metres and one mile' (TAS-CAS, 2018b). As noted above, the 400 m and 800 m events were among the five identified in Bermon and Garnier's IAAF/WADA-funded report (2017) as those in which women with high testosterone experienced an advantage. Since Chand competed in 100 m and 200 m sprints, these new regulations would not apply to her. Caster Semenya's events are the 800 m and 1500 m, both falling in the range targeted in the IAAF's draft regulations, although Bermon and Garnier did not find a significant testosterone advantage for women in the 1500 m event. It seems likely that the IAAF is attempting to cast a wide enough net to capture middle distance runners like Semenya regardless of the 'objective science' requirement.

4.5. TRANSGENDER POLICIES

The IOC's earliest policy on transgender athletes, the Stockholm Consensus, came into effect for the 2004 Athens Olympics. It required that the athlete's gender had been legally recognized, and that surgery, as well as two years of post-operative hormone therapy, had been completed. As with most Olympic industry initiatives, the policy was out of step with prevailing medical and societal views of the issue, and was the subject of extensive critique (see, for example, Cavanagh & Sykes, 2006; Teetzel, 2006).

In November 2015, the IOC released the report of the IOC Consensus Meeting on Sex Reassignment and Hyperandrogenism, which recommended that gender reassignment surgery and legal changes to gender identity should no longer be required for eligibility. Men would be allowed to compete without restriction, while, for women, serum testosterone would need to be at a specified low level (10 nmol/L) for 12 months before competition and throughout their competitive careers. So-called normal levels for females are 0.01–2.8 nmol/L, and above 10.5 nmol/L for males, according to the 'scientific consensus' cited by the IAAF. (The abbreviation nmol/L refers to nanomoles per liter; a nanomole is one billionth of a mole, which is an amount of a substance that contains a large number, six followed by 23 zeros, of molecules or atoms.) Only female athletes who have testosterone levels below the 'normal male range' or who have androgen insensitivity syndrome may compete in women's events. The 2015 policy stated: 'To require surgical anatomical changes... is not necessary to preserve fair competition and may be inconsistent with developing legislation and notions of human rights,' a rare nod to athletes' rights (IOC, 2015b, 1.E). However, some critics interpreted this dramatic change of policy as a ploy aimed at diverting public attention from other ongoing controversies over gender and eligibility (Brown, 2015).

Although it may have appeared to be innovative on the surface, the new policy reinforced the longstanding view of the male athlete as the 'gold standard.' Whereas a female-to-male (FTM) transgender athlete was apparently presumed to pose no threat to 'fair competition' and could compete without restrictions, rigid rules applied to male-to-female (MTF) women. The possibility that FTM athletes may have an 'unfair' advantage in the (admittedly few) sports where success rests on flexibility and grace as well as speed and strength – some components of gymnastics, figure skating, and diving, for example – was not contemplated.

Sport has long been a magnet for binary thinking when transgender rights are at stake. In 2013, during debates in the Canadian Parliament, Conservative politicians made a last-ditch but unsuccessful attempt to exclude sport from amendments to the Canadian Human Rights Act and the Criminal Code relating to gender identity. In February 2013, during debate on Bill C-279, they attempted to limit human rights protections to transgender Canadians by allowing the Ministry of State for Sport, Sport Canada and other sports governing bodies special powers 'to establish eligibility criteria for competing in events under [their] jurisdiction.' Liberal politician Irwin Cotler aptly dismissed the move as 'frivolous […] as if to contain some fictional mass of men trying to compete in women's sports, and vice versa […]' (Cotler, 2013).

Conservative lawmakers in Victoria, Australia, succeeded where their Canadian counterparts had failed. The 2010 Victoria Equal Opportunity Act, Section 72, included a long list of exceptions for 'competitive sporting activities,' allowing sports organizations to discriminate on the basis of sex or gender identity when the 'strength, stamina or physique of competitors is relevant,' in other words, virtually all sports except the small number that rely on kinesthetic expression. In 2017, Hannah Mouncey, a transgender football player, was excluded from the national women's competition. Although she satisfied IOC requirements in terms of testosterone levels, the conservative Victorian law better served the Australian Football League's purposes (Victorian Equal Opportunity, 2010).

Clearly, outdated binary thinking continues to shape popular misconceptions and prejudices, with damaging consequences for gender-variant women. In a 2017 example, an

Australian newspaper provided a platform for one uninformed sport administrator to voice his views on a transgender competitor. According to this Weightlifting Australia official, 'We're in a power sport which is normally related to masculine tendencies... where you've got that aggression, you've got the right hormones, then you can lift bigger weights,' he claimed (Commonwealth Games, 2017). He was objecting to the inclusion of New Zealander Laurel Holland, who, according to the media coverage, had satisfied IOC requirements and was eligible to compete as a woman. In the view of this official, after Holland 'suddenly' transitioned to female, she retained all the psychological advantages she had enjoyed as a man. In reality, the IOC requires evidence of appropriate testosterone levels for at least 12 months before competition, and, beyond that, the transition for individuals in New Zealand requires a medical evaluation, a period of 'real-life experience,' psychotherapy, cross-hormone treatment, possible surgery, and at least one year of medical monitoring (Ministry of Health, 2012). None of this is sudden, and the psychological costs before, during, and after the transition are significant.

4.5.1. Kristen Worley

The case of Canadian cyclist Kristen Worley demonstrates the injustices that arise from current WADA and IOC policies on testosterone. Worley struggled for more than 10 years to achieve justice for XY women in sport (males who have transitioned to become females, having XY chromosomes). Her challenges began when, as a competitive cyclist who had transitioned, she had a level of testosterone in her blood sample that exceeded that allowed for female athletes. As an XY woman, she had completed all the steps required to compete in women's competition (which under the IOC's original policy included surgery), and produced no natural testosterone. Her medical reports clearly showed that her body needed a certain level for her overall health. She experienced a number of problems, including muscle atrophy, and training for high performance sport became impossible. In 2006, facing this predicament, Worley applied to the Canadian Centre for Ethics in Sport (CCES) for a therapeutic use exemption (TUE) for synthetic testosterone in order to recover her health and resume training. It took three years for CCES to grant the exemption, which was only in effect for one year, and Worley was required to have blood tests every two months, contrary to WADA's usual required maximum of two tests per year.

In 2011, when Worley applied to CCES for an updated TUE, she was subjected to invasive gender verification and psychological testing. As she explained, 'I had to sit in front of a panel of men, and in conference calls with men I had never met [...] [answering questions] about my physiology and about the reasons why I wanted to compete in sport.' Her gynecological information was shared among male sports leaders as well as doctors. As she stated, 'It is a form of interrogation, rape and humiliation' (cited in Brown, 2015).

In contrast to the barriers Worley faced in her attempts to be granted TUEs, more than 100 athletes who competed in the 2016 Rio Olympics, that is, about 9%, were permitted to take a variety of 'prohibited' substances. This information became public after the hackers known as the Fancy Bears gained access to WADA's previously confidential database. In 2015, WADA issued 1,330 TUEs, 48% more than the previous year, clear evidence, according to Swiss Olympic Medical Centre director, Gerald Gremion, of the potential for exploitation of the TUE system (Gremion, 2017).

Worley continued with the higher level of synthetic testosterone and attempted to renew her annual Ontario Cycling Association (OCA) membership and Union Cycliste Internationale (UCI) license. She requested exemption from the section on UCI's anti-doping, on the grounds that they did not take into account her health status and hormonal requirements as an XY woman. As her 2015 submission to the Human Rights Tribunal of Ontario (HRTO) explained, the anti-doping codes, gender verification processes, and TUE policies generated by WADA and the IOC, and enforced by international and national sports governing bodies, constituted discriminatory treatment (HRTO, 2015). The IOC, WADA, UCI, Cycling Canada (CC), and OCA were named in the original application.

In response, CAS filed documents with the Ontario Superior Court of Justice, alleging that it would violate Switzerland's jurisdiction for HRTO to accept her case, as well as undermining the independence of the IOC and the Olympic movement. The IOC also argued that HRTO was not competent to hear a case that concerned sporting rules. However, since Worley was not granted a UCI license, she had not signed the contract requiring her to bring disputes to CAS. Furthermore, she correctly argued that this was not a sport-related dispute, but a human rights issue. In 2016, HRTO proceeded with the claims against the cycling organizations, and a settlement was finally reached in September 2017.

Worley was successful in gaining a commitment from these organizations to support and advocate for XY female athletes and their human rights. Both OCA and CC agreed to review their policies and to establish standards and guidelines 'based in objective science, from available sources, including those outside the organization' (HRTO, 2017, 2a). In view of sports bodies' longstanding reliance on 'in-house' medical researchers whose studies they funded, this constituted another important step forward. On the issue of TUEs, it was agreed that applications should be assessed by 'medical personnel with subject-area expertise,' within consistent time frames and testing requirements. The cycling organizations made a commitment to solicit relevant Canadian sports governing bodies to convey advocacy messages to the IOC, the WADA and other international organizations. UCI also agreed to support these advocacy initiatives at the international level (HRTO, 2017). These were all ground-breaking commitments that could potentially change gender-related policies and practices in sport, as well as challenging the power of IFs and the IOC.

4.6. 'OBJECTIVE SCIENCE'?

The goal of generating policies based on 'objective science,' as identified in both the Chand decision and Worley settlement, is a challenging one. It is understandable that athletes who have been unjustly disqualified from competition as a result of unsupported assumptions and binary thinking about sex and gender would look to science as a more reliable basis for policy decisions. However, as pioneering feminist scientists demonstrated more than 50 years ago, science is not neutral, and it is certainly not gender-neutral.

Challenging the prevailing view of science as separate from society, feminist scientists of the 1970s and 1980s argued that it needed to be examined as a social activity, embedded in 'Western, bourgeois, and masculine projects' (Harding, 1986, p. 9; see also Hubbard, Henifin, & Fried, 1979). As in other science subfields, preoccupation with sex differences was a defining feature of exercise sciences research at that time, and the male gatekeepers of knowledge were unlikely to publish null findings (where no significant sex differences were found). Male athletic achievement was the yardstick by which both males and females were measured. Although considerable progress has been made in the last five decades, challenging biased research that promotes the primacy of testosterone in athletic performance continues to be a difficult task.

Psychologists Jeremy and Paula Caplan (2004, p. 27) developed a useful guide for identifying high and low bias motives for conducting sex difference research. High bias is evident when researchers assume that biological or social factors determine behavior, when they set out to confirm or dispel 'common knowledge' about different abilities, or when they simply want to get published. Low bias motives include understanding relationships between biology and behavior, investigating the impact of social factors or 'common knowledge' notions, and testing theories.

In addition to potential gender bias in research design, the reporting of results is also subject to differing interpretations and emphases, generated by the researchers themselves and/or by mainstream media, as seen in the IAAF's campaign to quantify the 'testosterone advantage.' Results of studies go unreported, partially reported, or summarized in a biased way to fit the agenda of a particular organization or media source. Misguided attempts at 'balance' prompt journalists to seek out counterviews that are not based on the valid scientific research. Scientists' attempts to simplify complex issues may also lead to incomplete or misleading media coverage, including claims of *causality* when the researchers have merely demonstrated an *association* between variables.

Debates over reliable doping detection methods illustrate some of these pitfalls. In a 2004 critique of doping tests, subtitled 'How does one teach anti-doping officials about evidence-based decision making?,' Berry and Chastain discussed several factors that made testosterone tests unreliable

(Berry & Chastain, 2004, p. 6). Drawing on methodology used in medical science research, they pointed out that inferences and diagnoses are based on the sensitivity, specificity, and inherent variability of the test, as well as on prior probability – that is, the prevalence of the disease. In contrast, in matters of doping, they point out that there is 'an inevitable subjective aspect of assigning a prior probability' of drug use, resulting, as they demonstrate, in significant numbers of athletes whose test results are inaccurate, either false-positives or false-negatives. A passing reference in a medical journal article illustrates Berry and Chastain's 'prior probability' point. Discussing the importance of diagnosing and treating PCOS in adolescent girls, Buggs and Rosenfield (2005, p. 684) identified conditions with similar symptoms, warning doctors that 'serious athletes are prone to anabolic steroid abuse.'

In a strongly worded statement concerning doping test reliability, Berry and Chastain concluded: 'The trade-off between finding an innocent person guilty and protecting the integrity of sport is *far from obvious* [...] But it seems unreasonable to impugn 1% or even a tenth of a percent of nonusers who happen to be tested' (Berry & Chastain, 2004, p. 7; emphasis added). Their position stands in stark contrast to the relentless emphasis on winning the fight against doping and leveling the playing field for 'real' women.

4.7. T/E TESTS AND RACIALIZED MEN

In addition to the focus on gender-variant female athletes, T/E testing has significant implications for some racialized men. Debates over T/E test reliability began in 2008, following a study conducted by a Swedish team (Schulze et al., 2008). This research involved 50 male volunteers, divided into groups according to three different genotypes of UBT2B17, which is the major catalyst of testosterone excretion. T/E test results following one injection of testosterone were found to be highly dependent on the subject's particular UBT2B17 genotype, with the high excretor group having 20 times higher average maximum increase, compared to the low excretor group, whose samples failed to reach the 4.0 level after the injection. Moreover, 14% of subjects in the high excretor group had T/E ratios above 4.0 even before they had received the testosterone injection. In short, the reliability of the T/E test was seriously flawed.

The report pointed to the strong probability of false-positive results in about 9% of a random population of young men, which, as the authors noted, was an obvious concern 'for the legal rights of the sportsman' as well as 'extra workload for the doping laboratories' (Schulze et al., 2008, p. 2505). Overall, the results of this WADA-funded study led the authors to conclude that the sensitivity and specificity of existing tests would be improved by taking genetic variation into account. The subjects were not high-performance athletes, no women were included, and there was no attempt to investigate the effects of ethnicity.

A 2009 Swiss study funded by FIFA (Strahm et al., 2009) investigated UBT2B17 further, using as subjects 171 male professional soccer players from six countries, who were classified as African, Asian, Caucasian, and Hispanic. The researchers addressed the specificity and sensitivity shortcomings of WADA's current T/E tests, which had 'non-specific thresholds.' As they stated, 'The determination of thresholds specific to the ethnicity *and/or* the genotype responsible for [T/E levels]... is expected to enhance the detection of testosterone misuse' (Strahm et al., 2009, p. 1127, emphasis added). The study was not designed to investigate ethnicity alone, nor was it seeking to establish an association between ethnicity and a certain genotype.

Although the results did confirm some association between ethnicities and thresholds, Strahm et al. found variations within the same ethnic group. They acknowledged that their 'subjective ethnic classification' should, in future studies, be replaced by 'strictly set apart close ethnic groups' rather than geographically diverse groups whose members share the same ethnic identity — 'Hispanic,' for example. Significantly, they noted that '[E]nvironmental, dietary or genetic effects could act independently or in concert,' and that their research was not designed to address those questions (Strahm et al. 2009, pp. 1128–1129). In fact, a 1998 study had investigated both genetic and environmental/dietary effects by comparing androgen production and metabolism in Chinese men (non-athletes) living in Beijing with Chinese and Caucasian men living in Pennsylvania. The results showed no significant differences on most parameters between the Pennsylvania Chinese and the Caucasians, while the Beijing Chinese had reduced testosterone production rates. These findings led the authors to suggest that environmental/dietary factors rather than genetic factors explained the differences between Chinese and Caucasian men (Santner et al., 1998).

Strahm et al. (2009, p. 1129) concluded that genotype-specific thresholds allowed for 'a significantly greater individualization of the T/E reference range than knowledge of the ethnicity of the athlete.' Based on this finding, they recommended that individualized reference ranges based on carbon isotope ratio analysis should be included in the endocrine module of the ABP. Similarly, in a 2016 WADA-funded study of elite male and female athletes, a team of Swedish researchers found that urine was a less reliable DNA source than blood for establishing genotype, and, like some earlier researchers, they recommended that individual baseline values be included in the ABP (Choong et al., 2017). Changes of this kind would improve the reliability of T/E tests.

4.8. TESTOSTERONE: MEDIA CONSPIRACY THEORIES

The relatively small number of studies on T/E ratio and ethnicities attracted little attention outside of clinical pharmacology circles until August 2013 with the publication of an article by Nick Harris in the conservative UK newspaper, the *Daily Mail*, and the release of journalist David Epstein's book *The Sports Gene*. The media-generated 'born-to-cheat' conspiracy theory provides a disturbing but unsurprising demonstration of the distortion of scientific research findings to fit mainstream suspicions of 'the other,' in this instance, male Asian athletes.

Based on Schulze et al.'s 2008 study, Epstein claimed that members of certain ethnic groups carried a gene that kept the T/E ratio 'naturally' low, a gene that he provocatively labeled the 'impunity gene variant' and the 'get-out-of-drug-testing-free gene' (Epstein, 2013, p. 148). Adding circumstantial fuel to the fire, Harris implied that Asians exploited the 'doping with impunity gene,' giving as his only evidence WADA's 2012 figures showing fewer positive drug tests coming from Asia than from non-Asian regions – but 'it may just be coincidental,' he added (Harris, 2013).

While Epstein's book devoted only about one half-page to this research, Harris's article, 'Born to cheat: how world class athletes can take drugs... and get away with it' amounted to more than 1,400 words. The accompanying photographs of 12 Black athletes, six with doping violations, and only one white (doping) athlete, Lance Armstrong, effectively reinforced the racist message (Harris, 2013). Harris reported on both the early studies (Schulze et al., 2008; Strahm et al., 2009), adding his own hyperbole about ethnic differences and ignoring the caveats that the original researchers had included. The groups reportedly most likely to carry this gene were Koreans (about 80%), Chinese, and Japanese (30–40%), followed by Africans (20%), while those least likely were Caucasians (10%) and Hispanics (7%). Harris's 'shocked and appalled' tone was achieved by his liberal use of epithets like 'staggering,' 'shocking,' and 'frustrating.' He described Epstein, a *Sports Illustrated* journalist, as 'an expert on genetics in sport' – this, despite Epstein's biography showing no training in human sciences, only in the unrelated areas of environmental science and astronomy.

In one of a small number of commentaries that challenged Harris's and Epstein's interpretations, *Toronto Star* sport and business reporter Morgan Campbell debunked their 'junk science' claims. For starters, he explained, a gene that occurs as frequently as this cannot be considered rare; 'Hispanic' is an imprecise term that could be considered an ethnic or a geographic category, but not a 'race'; and those of mixed ethnicities are not accounted for (Campbell, 2013). (The 2009 study by Strahm et al. had, in fact, identified the problem with classifying diverse groups of people as Hispanic or African, but Harris ignored this, and several later studies continued to perpetuate these errors.)

As Campbell argued, the significant numbers of individuals who carry this gene cannot and should not be labeled 'born to dope,' and to 'position Europeans as the default and everybody else as the "other"' creates false categories. In short, in relation to ethnicity, Harris's widely reprinted article presented inconclusive research findings in 'the most inflammatory and least informative way' (Campbell, 2013).

Consider, for example, how a non-Eurocentric report of the research might look: 'Studies show that Asians are more likely than non-Asians to have a gene that keeps the T/E ratio low, a difference that leads to difficulties in interpreting results of commonly used anti-doping tests as well as having implications for diagnosing prostate diseases. It is recommended that testing procedures be improved for greater accuracy.' (A 2006 study of Korean and Swedish men funded by WADA and the Swedish Cancer Society had, in fact, focused on treatment of prostate cancer as well as doping – see Jakobsson et al. (2006).)

While generally sharing Harris's interpretation, the *New York Times* (Kolata, 2008) and *The Economist* avoided inflammatory language and provided some context, as did a chapter in *Sport, Drugs and Law* (Healey, 2016, pp. 7–8). An article titled 'High hopes' (2008) in *The Economist* even suggested that innocent athletes could defend themselves against false positive test results by bringing a copy of their genetic profiles to the 2008 Beijing Olympics.

Over the next five years, mainstream media and sports 'experts' continued to exploit these findings for a variety of racist and geopolitical purposes, with most sources portraying them as evidence of a genetic 'license to dope your brains out' that favored non-Caucasian athletes (Wagner, 2013). In one notable exception, an online blogger, Nick Gullo, discussed society's widespread reluctance to accept the fact that some athletes have genetic advantages of the kind that Epstein's book presented, including the UGT2B17 gene. The idea of 'inborn talent,' he pointed out, is at odds with the American Dream and 'the role of sports-as-social institution' (Gullo, 2013). The Olympic industry trades on the meritocracy myth, with 'role model' athletes telling children and youth to 'believe in your dreams,' rather than 'find your strengths.'

Statistically, as many scientists have explained, the world's best athletes are simply 'outliers,' 'genetic anomalies,' and winners in the 'genetic lottery' (see, for example, Noakes, 2011; Savulescu et al., 2004). Genetic good luck produces the body type and the physical and psychological traits necessary for success in a specific sport. Equally significant are the complex sociological forces behind athletic excellence, including the vast socioeconomic disparities between the global North and South, as well as within western and developing countries. For the non-science community and the mass media, however, these arguments lacked the currency of racist conspiracy theories.

4.9. 'DISREPUTE' CHARGES

In addition to doping charges, many athletes caught 'behaving badly' – usually young men – have faced criminal charges and subsequent suspension, in some cases, before their guilt has been established in court. Contracts between athletes and NOCs often include 'morality clauses' aimed at controlling athletes' conduct, with imprecise references to bringing themselves and/or their sport into 'disrepute.' As in commercial contexts outside of sport, 'brand protection' is the main goal of the Olympic industry partners in these contracts. As Findlay observed, the employer usually ensures that it is 'the sole judge of whether conduct violates the language of the morality clause,' and sports organizations' policies that identify 'disrepute' are 'often vague and ill-defined and thus weak from a legal perspective' (Findlay, 2014).

Decades before CAS was set up, an incident at the 1964 Tokyo Olympics attracted international attention. Following a flag-stealing prank and other alleged misconduct on the part of four female swimmers, the Australian Swimming Union imposed severe penalties on the young women, reportedly to defend 'its good name and the reputation of its members' and 'its responsibility to parents...' (Duggan, 2012). Champion swimmer Dawn Fraser received a 10-year suspension from international competition, later reduced to four, for her misconduct. An alternative account of the reasons for her suspension suggested that, together with three of her teammates, aged 14–19, she had disobeyed the team manager's ban on joining in the opening ceremony. Two of the young swimmers then gave up competitive swimming, while Fraser was reinstated too late to compete in the 1968 Olympics. Perhaps an AHD or CAS appeal today may have had a fairer result in terms of proportionate penalties for Fraser and her teammates, although some recent decisions suggest that punitive measures remain popular in cases such as these, with 'role model' rhetoric a common rationale.

The small number of studies that have investigated 'disrepute' charges reveals that the majority of cases involve male athletes, even when the author tries to suggest otherwise. The footnote in sports lawyer Patrick George's article, for example, states: 'The term 'sportsman' is used instead of 'sportsperson' in this article and is to be taken as gender neutral' (George, 2009, p. 24). 'Sportsman' may be the so-called gender-neutral term commonly used in athletes' contracts to refer to both men and women, but, in practice, very few women have been found guilty of disrepute charges (Jonson, Lynch, & Adair, 2013; Kosla, 2001). Of the 179 published CAS decisions in the category 'Disciplinary (except doping),' about two-thirds involved men's football, and the majority of individual appellants in other sports were male.

One of the small number of women who appealed disciplinary sanctions, mostly without success, was French marathon swimmer Aurelie Muller. FINA had disqualified Muller after she had obstructed another swimmer at the end of the 10-km race at the Rio 2016 Olympics, misconduct that was termed 'anti-sportif' (unsporting) (JO 16/027). One other

case involved Romanian rhythmic gymnastics coach/judge/
administrator Irina Deleanu, whose verbal attack on another
country's gymnast during a TV interview 'plainly amounted to
anti-sport behavior,' according to the CAS decision (CAS,
2012/A/3041, S. 55). Dismissing her 'supposed apology' – the
claim that she had been misunderstood and misinterpreted –
CAS upheld the suspension and fine imposed by the international gymnastics federation.

There are several possible explanations for the small numbers of female appellants involving disciplinary matters. In
light of the differences between the nature of men's and
women's sports, most notably women's lower participation
in team/contact sports, there may be fewer opportunities for
on-field misconduct, while women's socialization may be
responsible for fewer incidents of aggression off-field.
Alternatively, when female athletes do receive sanctions based
on misconduct, they may choose to avoid the expense and
potential public exposure that appeals to CAS entail, and the
likelihood of a negative outcome when the respondent is a
major IF or sports organization.

4.9.1. Ross Rebagliati

In 1998, when Canadian skier Ross Rebagliati tested positive
for marijuana, the AHD panel did not disqualify him because
that particular drug was not on any list of banned substances.
(By 2004, marijuana had been added to WADA's prohibited
list.) Rebagliati relied on the rather flimsy defense that he had
been exposed to second-hand smoke at a party. According to
that decision, CAS was not empowered to act on a marijuana
charge, regardless of its illegality in some jurisdictions.

McLaren (2010) presented Rebagliati's case as an example
where 'the letter of the law' worked in the athlete's favor, but

he also noted the 'controversial' decision involving Andrea Raducan, a 17-year-old Romanian gymnast who was stripped of her medal at the 2000 Olympics. The team doctor had given her a cold remedy that contained pseudoephedrine, a banned substance which, she claimed, had no proven performance-enhancing effect. Regardless, the AHD panel applied the strict liability principle, but demonstrated some sympathy for her by not imposing a suspension.

Commenting on the Raducan case, Parry claimed that, regardless of what appeared to be 'very harsh and unjust outcomes for some individuals,' the strict liability principle was essential to protect other athletes and maintain fair competition as well as to eliminate any and all excuses. Like others who have been similarly penalized, Raducan gained no performance advantage, but Parry maintained that the goal of preserving fairness justified 'the instrumental use of these athletes in the service of deterrence' (Parry, 2006, p. 276). In other words, from an anti-doping perspective, public shaming and blaming constitute a useful scare tactic.

It is interesting to note that McLaren selected the Rebagliati decision to demonstrate the advantages of AHD hearings, pointing out that the speedy resolution of his case allowed him to avoid the 'stress and anxiety' of a lengthy appeal process. McLaren contrasted this case with an earlier controversy involving Canadian swimmer Sylvie Frechette that had taken 16 months to resolve. Frechette appealed against a judge's error during the 1992 Olympics, that is, before AHDs had been introduced to the Olympics (McLaren, 2010, p. 314). The comparison may hold in terms of showing improvement in the time required for dispute resolution, but a judging error and a marijuana charge are not equivalent.

4.10. DISREPUTE AND CRIMINALITY: SOME AUSTRALIAN EXAMPLES

In 2008, CAS upheld an Australian Olympic Committee's (AOC) decision to bar two athletes from competing in the 2008 Olympics. Both were facing criminal charges, one for drink driving and the other for a drunken assault. CAS agreed with the AOC that these men's serious misconduct, apart from the criminal charges, brought them into 'disrepute' (CAS, 2008/A/1574).

The ruling against Australian swimmer Nicholas D'Arcy resulted from his intoxication, involvement in a fight, and serious injury to his victim. Putting aside any criminal allegations, the first CAS panel found that this behavior breached D'Arcy's membership contract with the AOC, specifically the Ethical Behaviour By-law stating that the athlete 'must not, by [his] acts or omissions, engage or participate in conduct which, if publicly known, would be likely to bring ... [him] into disrepute or censure' (CAS, 2008/A/1539, S. 6: 2).

D'Arcy followed up, unsuccessfully, with an application to the CAS Appeals Division. This decision included a lengthy paragraph of somewhat paternalistic speculations on the 'likely impact' of D'Arcy's inclusion as 'part of a large group of athletes... travelling overseas as a united body of representatives of his country and living together...' It noted, in particular, that the AOC Executive's input 'must be given great weight' because it had particular 'knowledge and experience' concerning the problems that his presence would cause to his teammates and to 'those involved in the *management* and organization of such a large group of diverse athletes ...' (CAS, 2008/A/1574, S. 50, emphasis added). The next section cited 'voluminous' critical media reports, some unproven but 'a considerable number' substantiated by admitted fact, that supported the charge of 'disrepute.' CAS appeared to justify

D'Arcy's exclusion from the team in part for pragmatic reasons, that is, the avoidance of management problems and negative public opinion. Referring specifically to the Wednesbury test of reasonableness, the panel dismissed D'Arcy's submissions that the AOC decision was disproportionate and 'irrational,' terming the behavior 'serious misconduct' that formed 'an ample basis' for the AOC's decision to terminate his membership.

Commenting on the D'Arcy case, sports lawyer Antoine Duval pointed out that, had the AOC contract failed to include a 'misconduct' provision, an athlete may have reasonably expected to retain his/her place. On the question of selection disputes, Duval was critical of CAS's reluctance to challenge 'the very wide scope of discretion of the NFs [national federations] and NOCs,' particularly in relation to decisions that clearly showed 'procedural deficiencies' (Duval, 2016, pp. 63, 66). Indeed, since one of CAS's functions is to promote 'best practice' and good governance on the part of IFs and NOCs, these deficiencies may bring 'disrepute' to CAS and its arbitrators. It is not clear how CAS might remedy this situation, since its main function is to determine whether the rules laid down by sports bodies have been followed, and not to assess the validity or fairness of such rules.

In 2012, when D'Arcy's behavior again attracted international attention, it appeared that the deterrent effects of harsh penalties invoked by the AOC and CAS were overestimated. While en route to the London Olympics via the US, he and a teammate posed with guns for a Facebook post. The AOC initially threatened to send them back to Australia for bringing the sport into disrepute, but then relented and allowed them to travel with their families and to compete. Following numerous behavior problems among the swim team, in particular the male swimmers at the London 2012 Olympics, Swimming Australia held an inquiry, with subsequent changes including a ban on alcohol, sleeping pills and gambling in the athletes' village.

The AOC banned Australian cyclist Chris Yongewaard from the Beijing 2008 Olympics following two drink driving criminal charges that caused serious injury to another cyclist. Yongewaard's contract included a signed declaration that he had 'not engaged at any time in conduct which is publicly known and in the absolute discretion of the President of the AOC [...] has brought or would be likely to bring me, [...] into disrepute or censure [...].' As in the D'Arcy case, the CAS panel, all Australian arbitrators, ruled that the punishment met the reasonableness principle. On the question of 'publicly known' conduct, they accepted the claim that media reports had made the charges widely known, but added that this 'does not, in our view, negate that the public would also realize the charges are allegations to be proven at trial (a fact also acknowledged in the letter of the AOC and the President)' (CAS, 2008/A/1605, S. 13). Finally, they added some Australia-specific prescriptive content concerning an athlete's responsibilities:

> *An athlete nominated for the Australian Olympic*
> *Team is presumed to be a person of good repute.*
> *He/she is perceived as both a leader and a role*
> *model within the Australian community. The*
> *Appellant has to answer two serious criminal*
> *charges. He faces severe statutory penalties if found*
> *guilty. The presumption of innocence is no answer*
> *to a determination by an AOC Selection Committee*
> *that the Appellant has, by particular conduct,*
> *brought himself into disrepute and therefore is*
> *found not eligible for selection to the Australian*
> *Olympic Team. (2008/A/1605, S. 19)*

In another 'disrepute' case, Australian shooter Michael Diamond was banned from the 2016 Rio Olympics for drink driving. In Diamond's defence, his lawyers argued that the AOC, exercising its discretion in such matters, had recently allowed field hockey player Anna Flanagan to compete at Rio after investigating her failure to disclose a drink driving charge to the hockey association, as required in her contract. Unsurprisingly, since a clause in the AOC Selection By-laws gave the president absolute discretion on selection disputes, the AOC felt no need to justify this apparent inconsistency (Diamond ineligible, 2016).

Overall, definitions of 'disrepute' and implicit assumptions about athletes' 'role model' responsibilities appear too imprecise and subjective to carry much weight in court. This is not to suggest that D'Arcy, Yongewaard, or others should have been eligible to compete in the Olympics, but rather to point out that Australian authorities' reliance on moral grounds may have resulted in harsher penalties for Australian athletes than for their non-Australian counterparts. Furthermore, as George (2009, p. 26) noted, since cricket, football, and swimming are particular sources of national pride for Australians, these celebrity sportsmen are more likely to be elevated to 'role model' status than their counterparts in less popular sports.

4.11. ROLE MODELS, 'RACE'/ETHNICITY, AND GENDER

On the issue of 'off-field' misconduct, a 2011 Canadian case involved a member of the national water polo team, Nathan Kotylak. Water Polo Canada suspended him for two years after photographs of his acts of vandalism during the Vancouver Stanley Cup riot were widely distributed on social media. Kotylak was warned, '[…] you're an athlete and you're representing Canada all the time, whether you're on the field of play […] or in the general public' (Canadian water polo, 2011). Most media accounts emphasized his age, referring to 'teen athlete' and 'rioting teen' in an attempt to downplay his misconduct, presumably because a 17-year-old Canadian male is not typically required to be a moral exemplar.

As I have argued elsewhere (Lenskyj, 2012, 2017), the 'celebrity athlete as role model' concept is largely a result of marketing efforts to attach an athlete's name to a sponsor's product. There is little if any evidence to support the claim that a high performance athlete is by definition a moral exemplar for children and youth, a well-rounded individual with a balanced life involving work, play, family and community. Furthermore, athletes do not necessarily 'sign on' to serve as positive examples, even if, as individuals, they are interested in inspiring young people. Professional athletes are workers, and their jobs are not always glamorous: they are expected to train hard, obey the rules and win medals.

In a 2012 commentary on racism in Australian sport, investigative journalist/filmmaker John Pilger compared D'Arcy's fate with that of Aboriginal boxer Damien Hooper, both of whom were participants in the 2012 London Olympics. D'Arcy had shown no remorse, and by declaring bankruptcy, had avoided paying damages to his victim. Hooper's alleged offense was to wear a T-shirt bearing the Aboriginal flag when he entered the ring, thereby making a political statement prohibited by the Olympic Charter. The AOC ordered Hooper to make a public apology – as Pilger termed it, 'a profanity in keeping with the enduring humiliation of the Aboriginal people' (Pilger, 2012).

Twelve years earlier, the same flag flew at Olympic venues during Sydney 2000, and Aboriginal sprinter Cathy Freeman ran a victory lap carrying both Australian and Aboriginal flags after her gold medal win. In combination with her role as the athlete chosen to light the Olympic cauldron, Freeman became the symbol of the supposed reconciliation between Black and white Australia (Lenskyj, 2002, chapter 3). The stark contrast in official and public responses to Freeman and Hooper points to the longstanding practice on the part of the dominant culture to divide athletes into 'good' and 'bad' Blacks or Aboriginals, with those in the 'bad' category blamed for bringing racial politics into sport.

In 2016, another misconduct charge involved American speed skater Michael Whitmore, who was involved in an alter-cation that resulted in serious injury to a Dutch skating coach, Stefano Donagrandi. The International Skating Union (ISU) found Whitmore guilty of misconduct and violation of its Code of Ethics, and imposed a one-year suspension, which he appealed. Both ISU and CAS rejected his argument that, because the brawl did not occur during an actual ISU activity, it was not subject to the ISU Code. In fact, the Code included numerous behaviors likely to occur outside sporting venues, including harassment, discrimination, exploitation, corruption, and doping-related violations. Similar to the Australian 'role model' rationale, ISU asserted that 'Improper behaviour can impair the values of the ISU and its reputation [...]' (CAS, 2016/A/4558, S. 54). CAS found sufficient evidence to prove physical violence and injury, conduct that 'brought the skating sport and the ISU into disrepute' (S. 80), but considered the suspension disproportionate and reduced it to six months.

Reflecting the desire to keep sport disputes 'within the family,' or in this case, 'within the brotherhood,' witnesses referred to Whitmore's verbal apology to Donagrandi, and the fact that the two men hugged and shook hands. Furthermore, Donagrandi was reported to have accepted the apology, stating 'that he only wanted to keep it among the individuals in that room' (S. 9) and 'had no intention of making more of the incident' (S. 12). On second thoughts, after hearing of the ISU's relatively lenient disciplinary measures, Donagrandi had reported the attack to the police, and the Dutch skating association filed a complaint to ISU on his behalf.

In a 2009 CAS case, Luis Suárez and FC Barcelona challenged FIFA's four-month ban on Suárez following a biting incident. Interestingly, the CAS decision made no reference to 'disrepute,' perhaps because it would take more than biting to threaten the reputation of this sport. The panel pointed to the player's recidivism and firmly rejected the argument that his 'remorse and apologies,' issued after disciplinary proceedings had started, should be considered as a mitigating factor (CAS, 2014/A/3665, 3666 & 3667).

Examining the 'disrepute' question, Sydney lawyers Tom Johnson and James Skelton argued that athletes and sports bodies must establish that the conduct itself, and not the 'peripheral sideshow' generated by 'speculative' media accounts, was responsible for this outcome. Commenting on the D'Arcy decision, they concluded that 'there is certainly a lower threshold to establish that an athlete has brought him or herself into disrepute' (Johnson & Skelton, 2016). They compared this case to the CAS decision on Mikhaylo Zubkov, a Ukrainian swim coach charged with bringing the sport, not himself, into disrepute, as a result of a filmed physical altercation with his daughter, a member of the swim team that he coached. CAS reduced Zubkov's six-year suspension, imposed by FINA, to eight months, citing the lack of evidence that his actions affected the sport of swimming. In fact, it was argued that FINA and the broadcaster contributed to the 'disrepute' by airing the footage (CAS, 2007/A/1291).

In D'Arcy's case, the first CAS panel stated that 'a reasonable member of the public,' having seen media accounts of the incident, 'would think considerably less of the Appellant on account of his conduct' (CAS, 2008/A/1539, S. 8). In both the D'Arcy and the Zubkov cases, it would be difficult to separate the conduct from the subsequent, often sensationalized, media coverage of that conduct. On the other hand, a 24-hour news cycle, supplemented by social media, is a twenty-first-century reality that athletes, coaches and SGBs should recognize.

Johnson and Skelton concluded by presenting a recent case in which they had represented an unnamed Australian professional athlete (most likely a football player) whose conduct had allegedly brought the sport into disrepute. The sports body had brought these charges months after the incident, during which time the athlete had continued to perform well on and off the field. At the code of conduct tribunal hearing, the lawyers successfully argued that, rather than the athlete's actual conduct, 'any subsequent poor reflection of the game was brought about... by the ensuing media attention... much of which contained speculation, as well as the governing body's general handling of the matter,' a timely warning for sport administrators who use the media to sway public opinion. Johnson and Skelton alerted athletes to the fact that individual sports such as swimming and athletics often included clauses regarding disrepute that the athlete has brought upon him/herself, charges that were easier for a governing body to establish than the broader concept of bringing the sport into disrepute (Johnson & Skelton, 2016).

Taking a different perspective on the misconduct issue, Kosla (2001) argued that an athlete's misconduct could more readily be seen to bring the sport into disrepute if that sport's governing body had named him/her as a role model, an argument along the lines of 'the bigger they are, the harder they fall.' This implies a double standard: should an athlete who has not been granted role model status receive more lenient treatment than one who has? Furthermore, a sports body's selection of role models may be motivated as much by pragmatic, commercial concerns as by ethical considerations. For example, the American National Football League has shown little interest in nominating Colin Kaepernick as a role model, or even in signing him, but there is no doubt that he has taken an ethical position as an anti-racist activist, and as such is a moral exemplar.

While it is clear that media coverage of athletes' misconduct tends to sensationalize the incident, a different 'boys will be boys' approach was offered by sports reporter Michael Pavitt. Writing for the website <insidethegames.biz > in a 2017 opinion piece titled 'No Need for Crackdown on Athletes' Freedom Despite Evening Exploits,' Pavitt referred to recent UK controversies involving cricketer Ben Stokes and football players Sergio Aguero and Wayne Rooney. These men had merely been having 'an evening out' before big games when something had 'gone wrong,' in one case a brawl, in another, drink driving, and in the third, an accident involving the player's taxi. Pavitt claimed that athletes' lifestyles are their own choices, and that these men's socializing would not have attracted attention if nothing had 'gone wrong' (Pavitt, 2017). In other words, in the drink driving and the brawl cases, the men were just unlucky to get caught. It is difficult to imagine a 'girls will be girls' rationale for similar behavior.

When the Canadian women's ice hockey team defeated the Americans at the Vancouver 2010 Winter Olympics, players were roundly criticized in the media and elsewhere for holding an on-ice celebration with beer, champagne, and cigars after the game had ended. One of the players was a month under the legal drinking age in the province of British Columbia. The team, along with Hockey Canada, issued their apologies, while the Canadian Olympic Committee distanced itself, assuring the public that it had not provided the alcohol or condoned the party. Team captain Hayley Wickenheiser pointed out that male hockey players, including 18-year-olds, traditionally celebrated by 'spraying champagne all over the dressing room,' with no public outrage, while Canadian IOC member Dick Pound considered the response to be 'like killing a mouse with an elephant gun' (IOC rep, 2010). At the same Winter Olympics, when Canadian gold medalist Jon Montgomery celebrated his victory in the men's skeleton event by downing a pitcher of beer as he walked through Whistler Village, he was described in one media account as a blue-collar 'folk hero' taking 'a euphoric, charming, boozy victory stroll' (MacIntyre, 2010). Videos of the beer episode remained on YouTube eight years later.

4.12. CONCLUSION

Within the IOC, WADA, IAAF, and CAS, institutions in which white men hold the greatest power, dated binary thinking about sex differences, gender, and gender variance, overlaid with prejudiced assumptions about racialized men and women, has generated countless situations where the lives and livelihoods of athletes have suffered. With a few notable exceptions (possibly, the pending case of Dutee Chand), the 'stacked decks' problem at CAS has made it a largely ineffective route for these athletes to resolve disputes. Suspicions of doping and complaints about athletes who are not 'real women' routinely set into motion a series of procedures based on the presumption of guilt – all clear violations of human rights. So powerful is the principle of sport exceptionalism that Europe's top human rights court has decreed that the admittedly intrusive provisions of WADA's whereabouts system are justified as weapons in the fight against doping. Similarly, sport's longstanding obsession with celebrity role models has proven a double-edged sword, rewarding with lucrative sponsorships those athletes 'fit for purpose,' punishing conduct that damages the brand, and reaffirming the sexual double standard on 'disrepute' charges.

CONCLUSION

Eighteen years ago, in the final chapter of my first book on the Olympic industry (Lenskyj, 2000, p. 195), I wrote, '[...] people who enjoy sport and value democracy would be ill-advised to support any aspect of the Olympics [...] their energies and talents would be better directed towards other regional, national and international sporting competitions that are currently conducted in more ethical and less exploitative ways.' Events of the last 18 years have done nothing to change my position on these issues, nor have my current findings on gender, sports law and CAS.

As in other sectors of society, women and members of ethnic minorities are generally more vulnerable than their white male counterparts to the vagaries of sports law, most notably its lack of transparency, unpredictability, constraints on access to domestic courts, the strict liability principle, and forced arbitration. Furthermore, the racism, sexism and homophobia underlying the mistreatment and abuse of gender-variant women at the hands of sport administrators and health professionals is a human rights issue that must be addressed. For their part, the mass media have largely collaborated with the Olympic industry to promote sport exceptionalism, while condemning 'drug cheats' and female athletes who are 'not woman enough.'

5.1. REFORM OR REVOLUTION?

In 2015, sports law scholar Antoine Duval provided an incisive critique of CAS titled 'The Court of Arbitration for Sport after Pechstein: Reform or revolution.' He included a comprehensive list of recommendations for reform that would address a raft of chronic problems, including lack of independence and transparency, governance problems, arbitrators' conflict of interest and repeat nominations, the closed list issue, and legal aid (Duval, 2015). Writing in the aftermath of Claudia Pechstein's legal battles, Duval, a senior researcher in European and international sports law at the Asser Institute in The Hague, noted that a CAS press release regarding Pechstein had asserted it was 'always prepared to listen and analyse the requests and suggestions' of stakeholders in order to 'continue its development with appropriate reforms' — an empty gesture at best, in view of its history. As the preceding discussion has demonstrated, there is little evidence of any serious steps towards reform since 1993, and ICAS and CAS have generally ignored the trenchant advice of critics such as Duval, Rigozzi, McArdle, and others, who have not only provided careful analyses of structural problems, but have also offered detailed recommendations for reform.

Of course, ICAS and CAS are only two of the players at the top level of the Olympic industry, and the other two formidable forces — the IOC and WADA — have their own agendas that are not necessarily compatible with a movement towards athletes' rights and social justice. With waning global interest in bidding for the Olympics and the IOC's credibility crisis vis-à-vis the Russian doping scandal, the Olympic industry's top priority in 2018 is brand protection, in order to maintain a 'product' that attracts global corporate sponsorships and future bids. Echoing 'clean sport' and 'level playing field' rhetoric, CAS decisions that appear to take a firm stand on doping athletes and on women with an alleged 'testosterone advantage' fit well with these priorities. The 2015 Interim Award in Dutee Chand's case threatened to disrupt this convenient arrangement, but it appears that the IAAF's revised regulations on hyperandrogenism will at least keep up appearances, by excluding some women from some events.

Duval (2015) concluded by predicting that, with scandals surrounding FIFA and the IAAF, 'global sport is at a turning point... it is truly about "reform or revolution".' In 2018, global sport remains vulnerable, but Duval's predicted revolution has failed to materialize, and steps towards reform have been minimal. Sport exceptionalism continues to thrive, virtually unchecked, and dispute resolution remains for the most part 'in the family of sport,' an arrangement that suits Olympic industry interests, regardless of the cost to individual athletes. The so-called war on doping, a losing battle against performance-enhancing drugs, continues to risk penalizing innocent athletes while others evade detection.

In my earlier analysis of the bribery scandals (Lenskyj, 2000), I proposed that the Olympic industry be dismantled, given the evidence of systemic corruption, lack of transparency and accountability, and resistance to change. Similarly, CAS's shortcomings, as documented here, suggest that mere reform is inadequate, and that more radical solutions are needed.

Instead of employing the *lex sportiva*/global sports law model, sport should follow best practice in international commercial arbitration. Mandatory arbitration clauses should be removed from contracts, and athletes should have recourse to national courts when arbitration fails to protect their human rights. The strict liability principle in doping cases needs to be abandoned, drugs unrelated to performance enhancement removed from the prohibited list, and changes made to prevent abuses of the TUE system. These are only some of the necessary first steps required to make dispute resolution in sport more equitable.

On the specific issues of doping, hyperandrogenism, and gender variance, IOC, WADA and IAAF should follow the lead of other sectors of society —public health, for example — using non-partisan researchers to develop evidence-based policy rather than relying on in-house experts to generate policy-based evidence in order to legitimize the Olympic industry's agenda.

5.2. AN END TO SPORT EXCEPTIONALISM

It is difficult to find any parallels to sport exceptionalism in other social contexts. Imagine, hypothetically, if the arts were similarly mythologized, with young men and women who are gifted in music, dance, or the visual arts mistreated in the same manner as athletes. Rather than celebrating their genetic gifts, hard work, and commitment, the organizations that control arts activities introduce stringent regulations governing every aspect of artists' lives — punitive rules that are based on suspicion rather than trust. The onus is on the artists to prove that they do not have an 'unfair' advantage because of their gender identity, skin color, or special genetic makeup. Their less successful peers complain about unfairness when these outliers achieve better results than they do, and many of these complaints eventually lead to appeals heard by a special tribunal, the Court of Arbitration for the Arts, that has close connections with arts governing bodies, and is staffed by arbitrators with arts experience. This arrangement is explained as 'user friendly' and efficient when it is, in fact, punitive and dangerous.

In addition, artists who excel in their fields are assumed to have relied on pharmaceutical aids, and are subjected to random testing to prove that their impressive abilities are not drug-assisted, but are the result of hard work and dedication. Again, the artist accused of cheating has no legal recourse apart from the special arts tribunal. Outside of the arts, the reliability of the relevant drug tests is the subject of extensive scientific debate and controversy, but the arts governing organizations have widespread media and public support for their zero tolerance policy and their testing programs. After all, according to their propaganda, everyone loves the arts and no one wants them tainted by unscrupulous artists and their questionable achievements. If these scenarios sound dystopian when applied to artists, they are obviously a threat to athletes' rights, and, more broadly, to the future of global sport.

CAS AWARDS AVAILABLE AT JURISPRUDENCE.TAS-CAS.ORG

TAS 92/63	G. v FEI
CAS 93/103	SC Langnau v LSHG
CAS 94/129	USA Shooting v International Shooting Union
CAS 94/132	Puerto Rico Amateur Baseball Federation v USA Baseball
CAS 98/208	N., J., Y., and W. v FINA
CAS2001/A/337	B. v FINA
CAS 2004/A/651	Mark French v Australian Sports Commission and Cycling Australia
OG/04/006	AOC v IOC and ICF
CAS 2005/A/990	P. v International Ice Hockey Federation
CAS 2007/A/951	Guillermo Canas v ATP Tour
CAS 2007/A/1291	Mikhaylo Zubkov v FINA
CAS 2007/A/1312	Jeff Adams v CCES
CAS 2008/A/1539	Nicolas D'Arcy v AOC
CAS 2008/A/1574	Nicolas D'Arcy v AOC
CAS 2008/A/1605	Chris Jongewaard v AOC
CAS 2009/A/1912-1913	Claudia Pechstein v ISU
CAS 2010/A/2230	International Wheelchair Basketball Federation v UKAD & Simon Gibbs

(*Continued*)

CAS 2011/A/2384	UCI and WADA v Alberto Contador Velasco and RFEC
CAS 2011/O/2422	USOC v IOC
CAS 2011/A/2658	BOA v WADA
CAS 2012/A/3041	Irina Deleanu v FIG
CAS 2014/A/3572	Sherone Simpson v JADCO
CAS 2014/A/3759	Dutee Chand v IAAF and Athletics Federation of India
CAS 2014/A/3665-3667	Luis Suárez, FC Barcelona and Uruguayan Football Association v FIFA
CAS 2015/A/3925	Traves Smikle v JADCO
CAS 2015/A/3899	F. v Athletics Kenya
CAS 2015/A/4129	Demirev, Enev, Filev, Ivanove, Maneva, Markov, Minchev, Muradiov, Nazif, Nguen, Urumov v IWF
CAS 2015/A/4095	Bernardo Rezende & Mario da Silva Pedreira Junior v FIVB
CAS 2016/A/4643	Maria Sharapova v International Tennis Association
CAS 2016/A/4501	Joseph Blatter v FIFA
CAS 2016/A/4558	Mitchell Whitmore v ISU
JO 16/027	Fédération Francaise de Natation, Aurelie Muller, Comité Nationale Olympique et Sportif Francais v FINA
CAS 2017/A/5110	FIS v Therese Johaug and the Norwegian Olympic and Paralympic Committee and Confederation of Sport
CAS 2017/O/5039	IAAF v Russian Athletic Federation and Anna Pyatykh
CAS OG 18/02	Victor Ahn et al. v IOC
CAS OG 18/03	Leghov et al. v IOC

SWISS FEDERAL TRIBUNAL AWARDS ENGLISH TRANSLATIONS AVAILABLE AT SWISSARBITRATIONDECISIONS. COM

SFT 4A_600/2010	Federation X v Federation A, B, C, D, E and F (17 March, 2011)
SFT 4A_640/2010	A. v WADA, FIFA and Cyprus Football Association (18 April, 2011)
SFT 4A_558/2011	Francelino da Silva Matuzalem v FIFA (27 March, 2012)

BIBLIOGRAPHY

Adair, D. (11 January, 2016). The pomp in circumstance: CAS rules against Essendon players. *The Conversation.* Retrieved from theconversation.com/the-pomp-in-circumstance-cas-rules-against-essendon-players-53043

Alleged illegal composition of arbitral tribunal. (23 September, 2008). *Swiss International Arbitrations Decisions.* Retrieved from swissdecisions.com/alleged-illegal-composition-of-arbitral-tribunal-lack-of-violi

Allegedly infra petita award. (23 June, 2009). *Swiss International Arbitrations Decisions.* Retrieved from swissdecisions.com/allegedly-infra-petita-award-violation-of-public-policy-and-of-r

Amnesty International. (2016). *Annual Report, China: 2015/16.* Retrieved from amnesty.org/en/countries/asia-and-the-pacific/china/report-china/

Anderson, J. (2000). 'Taking sports out of the courts': Alternative dispute resolution and the International Court of Arbitration for Sport. *Journal of Legal Aspects of Sport, 10*(2), 123–128.

Anderson, J. (2013). Doping, sport and the law: Time for repeal or prohibition? *International Journal of Law in Context, 9*(2), 135–159.

Another first for the Court of Arbitration for Sport.
(July–October, 2006). *International Sports Law Journal*,
3–4, 121–122.

Anti-doping study supported by IOC investigates incentives
to stop doping. (30 October, 2017). Retrieved from
University of Adelaide News & Events. adelaide.edu.au/
news/news95902.html

Antitrust: International Skating Union's restrictive penalties.
(8 December, 2017). *European Commission*. Retrieved from
europa.eu/rapid/press-release_IP-17–5184_en.htm

AOC culture out of step with Olympic ideals. (24 August,
2017). *The Australian*. Retrieved from theaustralian.com.au/
sport/Olympics/aoc-culture-out-of-step-with-olympic-ideal-
review-finds/news-story/d48485bf960fb4bc749231b0ca
41a611

Australian Sports Anti-Doping Authority (ASADA)
Amendment Bill. (2013). Parliament of the Commonwealth
of Australia. Retrieved from aph.gov.au/parlinfo/download/
legislation/bills/s902_aspassed/toc_pdf.1300920.pdf;
fileType=application%2Fpdf

Bach, T. (6 November, 2013). Statement on the occasion of
the adoption of the resolution 'Building a peaceful and better
world through sport and the Olympic ideal', UN General
Assembly. Retrieved from stillmed.olympic.org/Documents/
IOC_President/2013-11-6_Speech_IOC_President_Bach-
Olympic_Truce_adoption_Speech_4_November.pdf

Bairner, A., & Molnar, G. (Eds.). (2010). *The Politics of the
Olympics*. London: Routledge.

Beamish, R., & Ritchie, I. (2006). *Fastest, Highest, Strongest:
A Critique of High Performance Sport*. London: Routledge.

Beloff, M. (2012). Is there a *Lex Sportiva*? In R. Siekmann & J. Soek (Eds.), *Lex Sportiva: What Is Sports Law?* (pp. 69–89). The Hague: ASSER Press.

Bermon, S., et al. (2014). Serum androgen levels in elite female athletes. *Journal of Clinical Endocrinology & Metabolism*, *99*(11), 4328–4335.

Bermon, S. (2017). Androgens and athletic performance of elite female athletes. *Current Opinion in Endocrinology*, *24*(3), 246–251.

Bermon, S., & Garnier, P. (2017). Serum androgen levels and their relation to performance in track and field. *British Journal of Sports Medicine*, *51*(17), 1309–1314.

Berry, D., & Chastain, L. (2004). Inferences about testosterone abuse among athletes. *Chance*, *17*(2), 5–8.

Best, S. (11 October, 2017). Athletes should be fitted with microchips…. *Daily Mail*. Retrieved from mailonline/co.uk/sciencetech.article-4969122/Athletes-fitted-microchips-stop-doping.html

Blackshaw, I. (2003). The Court of Arbitration for Sport: An international forum for settling disputes effectively 'within the family of sport'. *Entertainment and Sports Law Journal*, *2*(2), 61–83.

Blackshaw, I. (July-October, 2006). Fair play on and off the field of play. *International Sports Law Journal*, *3–4*, 107–117.

Blackshaw, I. (July-October, 2007). The specificity of sport and the EU White Paper on sport: Some comments. *International Sports Law Journal*, *3–4*, 87–88.

Blackshaw, I. (2013). ADR and sport: Settling disputes through the Court of Arbitration for Sport. *Marquette Sports Law Review*, *24*(1), 1–58.

BOA get backing on lifetime bans. (27 January, 2012). *ESPN*. Retrieved from espn.co.uk/olympics/story/_/id/7510602/sebastian-coe-british-government-back-lifetime-olympic-doping-ban

Booth, D., & Tatz, C. (December, 1995). The big picture. *Inside Sport*, 14.

Bowen, J., Katz, R., Mitchell, J., Polden, D., & Walden, R. (2017). *Sport, Ethics and Leadership*. London: Routledge.

Boye, E., et al. (2017). Doping and drug testing. *EMBO Reports*, *18*(3), 351–354.

Brijnath, R. (9 May, 2017). Maria Sharapova deserves a second chance but must use it well. *The Straits Times*. Retrieved from straitstimes.com/sports/tennis/sharapova-deserves-a-second-chance-but-must-use-it-well

Brohm, J.-L. (1978). *Sport: A Prism of Measured Time*, trans I. Fraser. Ink Links.

Brown, A. (12 June, 2015). Sport's gender policies: An affront to human rights. *Sports Integrity Initiative*. Retrieved from sportsintegrityinitiative.com/sports-gender-policies-an-affront-to-human-rights/

Brown, A. (30 August, 2017). 'Official' publication of doping prevalence study IAAF tried to block. *Sporting Integrity Initiative*. Retrieved from sportsintegrityinitiative.com/official-publication-doping-prevalence-study-iaaf-tried-block/

Brownell, S. (2012). Commercialism, values and education in the Olympic movement today. In J. Parry & S. Brownell (Eds.), *Olympic Values and Ethics in Contemporary Society* (pp. 95–108). Belgium: Ghent University.

Brubaker, J., & Kulikowski, M. (2010). Sporting chance? The Court of Arbitration for Sport regulates arbitrator-counsel role switching. *Virginia Sport and Entertainment Law Journal*, *10*(1), 1–16.

Buggs, C., & Rosenfield, R. (2005). Polycystic ovary syndrome in adolescence. *Endocrinology and Metabolism Clinics of North America*, *34*(3), 677–705.

Bull, A. (July 30, 2012). Ye Shiwen's world record Olympic swim 'disturbing', says top US coach. *The Guardian*. Retrieved from guardian.co.uk/sport/2012/jul/30/ye-shiwen-world-record-olympics-2012

Butler, N. (2 November, 2017). Bach accuses critics of Olympic Movement of ignorance and aggression. *Inside the Games*. Retrieved from insidethegames/biz/articles/1057397/bach-accuses-critics-of-olympic-movement-of-ignorance-and-aggression

Byrnes, A. (2016). Human rights and the anti-doping lex sportiva. In U. Haas & D. Healey (Eds.), *Doping in Sport and the Law* (pp. 81–104). London: Bloomsbury.

Campbell, M. (30 August, 2013). Doping in sport: Are non-white athletes born to cheat? Retrieved from bymorgancampbell.com/2013/08/13/doping-in-sport-are-non-white-athletes-born-to-cheat/

Canadian water polo player suspended. (27 September, 2011). *Toronto Star*. Retrieved from thestar.com/sports/Olympics/2011/09/27/canadian_water_polo_player_suspended_two_years_for_role_in_stanley_cup_riot.html

Caplan, J., & Caplan, P. (2004). The perseverative search for sex differences in mathematics ability. In A. Gallagher & J. Kaufman (Eds.), *Gender Differences in Mathematics* (pp. 25–47). Cambridge: Cambridge University Press.

CAS award allocating fees and costs in violation of the right to be heard of parties. (17 March, 2011). *Swiss International Arbitrations Decisions*. Retrieved from swissarbitrationsdecisions.com/cas-award-allocating-fees-and-costs-in-violation-of-the-right-to

Casini, L. (2011). The making of a lex sportiva by the Court of Arbitration for Sport. *German Law Journal, 12*(5), 1317–1340.

Cavalieros, P. (2014). Can the arbitral community learn from the closed CAS system? Presentation to the Irish Arbitration Association Conference, Dublin. Retrieved from arbitrationconference.com/page/187/presentations-2014

Cavanagh, H., & Sykes, H. (2006). Transsexual bodies at the Olympics. *Body and Society, 12*(3), 75–102.

Chappelet, J.-L. (2016). Autonomy and governance. *Transparency International: Global Corruption in Sport* (pp. 16–28). London: Routledge.

Choong, E., et al. (2017). Discordant genotyping results using DNA isolated from anti-doping control urine samples. *Drug Testing and Analysis, 9*(7), 994–1000.

Coletta, A. (23 December, 2015). Kristen Worley, Canadian cyclist, faces IOC challenge in gender verification suit. *CBC Sports*. Retrieved from cbc.ca/sports/olympics/generic/kristen-worley-canadian-cyclist-faces-ioc-challenge-in-gender-verification-suit-1.3377266

Commonwealth Games: Backlash over New Zealand transgender weightlifter. (24 November, 2017). *Brisbane Times*. Retrieved from brisbanetimes.com.au/commonwealth-games-2018-backlash-over-new-zealand-transgender-weightlifter-laurel-hubbard-20171124-gzsgdq. html

Comsti, C. (2014). Metamorphosis: How forced arbitration arrived in the workplace. *Berkeley Journal of Employment & Labor Law*, 5(1/2), 6–31.

Coste, O. et al. (2011). Polycystic ovary-like syndrome in adolescent competitive swimmers. *Fertility and Sterility*, 96(4), 1037–1042.

Cotler, I. (27 February 2013). 'Debate, Bill C-279' Canadian Parliament. Retrieved from openparliament.ca/bills/41-1/C-279/

Cox, D. (August 7, 2017). Gatlin over Bolt makes track even harder to trust. *Toronto Star*. Retrieved from thestar.com/sports/amateur/2017/08/07/gatlin-over-bolt-makes-track-even-harder-to-trust-cox.html

de Hon, O., Kuipers, H., & van Bottenburg, M. (2015). Prevalence of doping use in elite sports: A review of numbers and sources. *Sports Medicine*, 45(1), 57–69.

De Marco, N. (4 July, 2016). Compelled consent – Pechstein & the dichotomy and future of sports arbitration, *Blackstone Chambers: News, cases and analysis*. Retrieved from blackstonechambers.com/news/analysis-compelled_consent_/

Department for Digital, Culture, Media and Sport. (24 August, 2017). *Review of Criminalisation of Doping in Sport*. Retrieved from gov/uk/government/publications/review-of-criminalisation-of-doping-in-sport

Diamond ineligible for nomination. (30 June, 2016). *Australian Olympic Committee*. Retrieved from corporate.olympics.com.au/6592E7F-950E-4135-9E4779D6B58975C4

Diaz, E., & Dockterman, E. (October 2016). The itsy-bitsy, teensy-weensy, tiny fine print that can allow sexual harassment to go unheard. *Time Magazine*, 33–35.

Dickerson, J. (25 August, 2015). International arbitration in sport, *Lawyer Issue*. Retrieved from lawyerissue.com/international-arbitration-in-sport-why-the-pechstein-case-could-throw-the-court-of-arbitration-for-sport-into-disarray/

Dimeo, P. (12 December, 2014). Tougher rules on drugs in sport won't help detect more doping. *The Conversation*. Retrieved from theconversation.com/tougher-rules-on-drugs-in-sport-wont-help-detect-more-doping-35404

Dismissal of an appeal …anti-doping…. (18 April, 2011). *Swiss International Arbitration Decisions*. 4A_640/2010. Retrieved from swissarbitrationdecisions.com/dismissal-of-an-appeal-to-set-aside-a-cas-award-a-reference-to-a

Dismissal of an appeal … lack of jurisdiction…. (13 February, 2012). *Swiss International Arbitration Decisions*. Retrieved from swissarbitrationdecisions.com/dismissal-of-an-appeal-to-set-aside-a-cas-award-on-the-grounds-o

Doping control: whereabouts requirement does not breach Convention. (18 January, 2018). European Court of Human Rights press. Retrieved from d3mjm6zw6cr45s.cloudfront.net/2018/01/Press-release-issued-by-European-Court-of-Human-Rights-on-Thursday-18th-January.pdf

Dreier, F. (17 July, 2013). Rule change on Olympic marijuana testing. *USA Today*. Retrieved from usatoday.com/story/sports/olympics/2013/07/17/ross-rebagliati-olympics-marijuana-drug-testing/2528283/

Drinkwater, B. (1984). Women's physiological response to exercise. *ICSSPE Review*, 7, 19–24.

Duggan, K. (30 June, 2012). Advance Australia's Fraser. *Irish Times*. Retrieved from irishtimes.com/sport/advance-australia-s-fraser-1.1069833

Duval, A. (2015). The Court of Arbitration for Sport after Pechstein: Reform or revolution? *Asser Sports Law*. Retrieved from asser.nl/SportsLaw/Blog/post/the-court-of-arbitration-for-sport-after-pechstein-reform-or-revolution

Duval, A. (2016). Getting to the games: The Olympic selection drama(s) at the court of arbitration for sport. *International Sports Law*, *15*(1/2), 52–66.

Duval, A., & Marino, G. (23 May, 2014). Quantifying the Court of Arbitration for Sport. *Asser Sports Law*. Retrieved from asser.nl/SportsLaw/Blog/post/quantifying-the-court of-arbitration-for-sport-by-antoine-duval-and-gianni-marino

Eichberg, H. (1998). *Body Cultures*. London: Routledge.

Eichberg, H. (2004). The global, the popular and the inter-popular: Olympic sport between market, state and civil society. In J. Bale & M. Christensen (Eds.), *Post-Olympism? Questioning Sport in the Twenty-First Century* (pp. 65–80). London: Berg.

Epstein, D. (2013). *The Sports Gene*. New York, NY: Penguin Random House.

Espy, R. (1979). *The Politics of the Olympic Games*. Berkeley, CA: University of California Press.

Fenichel, P. et al. (2013). Molecular diagnosis of 5a-reductase deficiency in 4 elite young female athletes through hormonal screening for hyperandrogenism. *Journal of Clinical Endocrinology & Metabolism*, *98*(6), E1055–E1059.

Ferguson-Smith, M., & Bavington, L. (2014). Natural
selection for genetic variants in sport. *Sports Medicine*,
44(12), 1629–1634.

Findlay, H. (2013). Gender and equality: *Sagen v VANOC*
[2009] BCCA 552. In J. Anderson (Ed.), *Leading Cases in
Sports Law* (pp. 353–367). The Hague: Asser.

Findlay, H. (6 March, 2014). You can't do or say that:
Constraining individual conduct in a public and commercial
world. *LawNow*. Retrieved from lawnow.org/you_cant_do_
or_say_that/

Ford, B. (2 March, 2017). Anti-doping reform needs more
urgency. *ESPN*. epsn.com/olympics/story/_/id/18797433/
olympians-michael-phelps-adam-nelson-stand-anti-doping-
reform-congressional-hearing

Former FIFA boss named in corruption case. (12 July, 2012).
Swissinfo. swissinfo.ch/eng/court-order-former-fifa-boss-
named-in-corruption-case/33091368

Foster, A. (6 August, 2017). Why was Justin Gatlin booed?
The Express. Retrieved from express.co.uk/sport/othersport/
837515/Justin-Gatlin-why-booed-Usain-Bolt-drug-cheat-
London-2017-doping-bans-World-Championships

Foster, K. (2003). Is there a global sports law? *Entertainment
Law*, *2*(1), 1–18.

Foster, K. (2005). Lex sportiva and lex ludica: The Court of
Arbitration for Sport's jurisprudence. *Entertainment and
Sports Law Journal*, *3*(2), 1–14. Retrieved from
entsportslawjournal.com/articles/10.16997/eslj/112/

Fridman, S. (1999). Conflict of interest, accountability and
corporate governance: The case of the IOC and SOCOG.
University of New South Wales Law Journal, *22*(3),

781–798. Retrieved from austlii.edu.au/au/journals/
UNSWLawJl/1999/28.html

Geeraert, A., Alm, J., & Groll, M. (2013). Good governance in international non-governmental sport organisations. In J. Alm (Ed.), *Action for Good Governance in International Sports Organisations* (pp. 190–218). Copenhagen: Danish Institute for Sport Studies/Play the Game.

Geeraets, V. (2017). Ideology, doping and the spirit of sport. *Sport, Ethics and Philosophy*, *11*, 1–17.

Genel, M. et al. (2016). The Olympic Games and athletic sex assignment. *JAMA*, *316*(13), 1359–1360.

George, P. (2009). Sport in disrepute. *Australian and New Zealand Sports Law Journal*, *4*(1), 24–54.

Giles, A., & Loeliger, J. (7 July, 2013). Australia: New powers for ASADA to investigate the use of drugs in sport. *Mondaq Law*. Retrieved from mondaq.com/australia/x/248992/Sport/New+powers+for+ASADA+to+investigate+the+use+of+drugs+in+sport

Gilligan, C. (1982). *In a Different Voice*. Cambridge, MA: Harvard University Press.

Greene, P. (2017). When athletes are wrongly sanctioned under the World Anti-Doping Code. *Maryland Journal of International Law*, *32*(1), 338–345.

Gremion, G. (2017). The governance of doping in sport. In G. Hendriks & J. Landrove (Eds.), *Collected Insights from the Field of Sport Vol. 3: Governance and Ethics* (pp. 35–44). Lausanne: International Academy of Sport Science and Technology.

Grinspan, L. (9 March, 2016). What a racket: Nike suspends Sharapova, but has stuck with men who do worse. *USA*

Today. Retrieved from college.usatoday.com/2016/03/09/
what-a-racket-nike-suspends-sharapova-but-has-stuck-with-
men-who-do-worse/

Growth Hormone 2004 Project. (2017). *GH-2004-Fighting
Growth Hormone misuse in sport*. UK: Southampton
University. Retrieved from southampton.ac.uk/gh2004/index.
page

Gullo, N. (24 September, 2013). Nick 'The Tooth' takes on
America's meritocracy myth. *Vice*. Retrieved from fightland.
vice.com/blog/nick-the-tooth-takes-on-americas-meritocracy-
myth

Hagmar, M. et al. (2009). Hyperandrogenism may explain
reproductive dysfunction in Olympic athletes. *Medicine &
Science in Sports and Exercise*, *41*(6), 1241–1248.

Harding, S. (1986). *The Science Question in Feminism*.
Ithaca NY: Cornell University Press.

Harris, N. (24 August, 2013). Born to cheat! *Daily Mail*.
Retrieved from dailymail.com.uk/sports/othersports/article-
2401478/How-world-class-athletes-drugs-away-it.html

Healey, D. (2016). The myth of the level playing field.
In Haas & Healey (Eds.), *Sport, Drugs and the Law*
(pp. 3–17).

Healy, M. et al. (2014). Endocrine profiles in 693 elite
athletes in the postcompetition setting. *Clinical
Endocrinology*, *81*(2), 294–305.

Henne, K. (2015). *Athlete Citizenship: Regulating Doping and
Sex in Sport*. New Brunswick, NJ: Rutgers University Press.

Hickie, T. (2016). Do what I say, not what I do. In Haas &
Healey (Eds.), *Sport, Drugs and the Law* (pp. 47–60).

High hopes. (3 April, 2008). *The Economist*. Retrieved from economist.com/node/10952799

Hill, J. (2009). The European Commission's White Paper on Sport: A step backwards for specificity? *International Journal of Sport Policy and Politics*, 1(3), 253–266.

Hruby, P. (3 August, 2016). The drugs won: The case for ending the sports war on doping. *Vice Sports*. Retrieved from sports.vice.com/en_ca/article/pgnamn/the-drugs-won-the-case-for-ending-the-sports-war-on-doping

Hubbard, R., Henifin, M., & Fried, B. (1979). *Women Look at Biology Looking at Women*. Cambridge, MA: Schenkman.

Human Rights Tribunal of Ontario. (2015). HRTO Applicant's Reply and Submission on Preliminary Issues: Kristen Worley v Ontario Cycling Association, Cycling Canada Cyclisme, International Olympic Committee and Union Cycliste Internationale.

Human Rights Tribunal of Ontario. (5 July, 2017). Kristen Worley v Ontario Cycling Association, Cycling Canada Cyclisme, Union Cycliste Internationale Minutes of Settlement.

Hunter, R., & Shannon, J. (2017). Athletes banned, athletes cleared, athletes reinstated. *Journal of Education and Social Policy*, 7(1), 8–21.

IAAF. (2011). *Regulations Governing Eligibility of Females with Hyperandrogenism to Compete in Women's Competition*. Retrieved from iaaf.org/search?q=hyperandrogenism

IAAF. (2013). *IAAF Competition Rules* 2014–2015. Retrieved from iaaf.org/about-iaaf-documents/rules-regulations

IAAF. (3 July, 2017). Levelling the playing field in female
sport. Retrieved from iaaf.org/news/press-release/
hyperandrogenism-research

Infantino, G. (2006). Meca-Medina: A step backwards for
the European Sports model and the specificity of sport?
UEFA. Retrieved from uefa.com/MultimediaFiles/Download/
uefa/KeyTopics/480391_DOWNLOAD.pdf

Ingle, S. (9 October, 2017). Inside British Bobsleigh's 'toxic'
culture. *The Guardian*. Retrieved from theguardian.com/
sport/2017/oct/09/british-bobsleigh-toxic-culture-uk-sport-
winter-olympics-2018

Institute of National Anti-Doping Organizations (iNADO)
Board of Directors. (23 March, 2017). Response to
International Olympic Committee (IOC) Declaration of
March 16, 2017. *Institute of National Anti-Doping
Organizations*. Retrieved from inaido.org/about/press-
releases.html

IOC. (1996). IOC World Conference on Women and Sport
Final Resolution. Retrieved from stillmed.olympic.org/media/
Document%20Library/OlympicOrg/Documents/Conferences-
Forums-and-Events/Conferences/IOC-World-Conferences-on-
Women-and-Sport/1st-IOC-World-Conference-on-Women-
and-Sport-Final-Resolution-Lausanne-1996.pdf

IOC. (November 2003). Statement of the Stockholm
Consensus on Sex Reassignment in Sports. stillmed.olympic.
org/Documents/Reports/EN.en_report_905.pdf

IOC. (2007). Preliminary Document: Basic Universal
Principles of Good Governance of the Olympic and Sports
Movement. Retrieved from stillmed.olympic.org/AssetsDocs/
importednews/documents/en_report_1292.pdf

IOC. (13 February, 2008). Olympic and sports movement discuss 'Basic Universal Principles of Good Governance'. Retrieved from olympic.org/news/olympic-and-sports-movement-discuss-basic-universal-principles-of-good-governance

IOC. (2015a). Olympic Charter. Retrieved from stillmed.olympic.org/Documents/olympic_charter_en.pdf

IOC. (November 2015b). IOC Consensus Meeting on Sex Reassignment and Hyperandrogenism. Retrieved from stillmed.olympic.org/Documents/Commissions_PDFfiles/Medical_commission/2015-11_ioc_consensus_meeting_on_sex_reassignment_and_hyperandrogenism-en.pdf

IOC. (16 March, 2017a). Declaration of the IOC Executive Board. Retrieved from olympic.org/news/declaration-of-the-executive-board-1

IOC. (1 November, 2017b). IOC sanctions two Russian athletes as part of Oswald Commission findings. Retrieved from olympic.org/news/ioc-sanctions-two-russian-athletes-as-part-of-oswald-commission-findings

IOC. (22 November, 2017c). IOC president at the Council of the European Union. Retrieved from olympics.org/news/ioc-president-at-the-council-of-the-european-union-for-meeting-on-sport-in-the-21st-century

IOC. (11 December, 2017d). Decision of the IOC Disciplinary Commission in the proceedings against Aleksandr Tretiakov. Retrieved from stillmed.olympic.org/media/Document%20Library/OlympicOrg/IOC/Who-We-Are/Commissions/Disciplinary-Commission/2017/SML-022-Decision-Disciplinary-Commission-Aleksandr-TRETIAKOV.pdf

IOC. (1 February, 2018a). IOC statement on CAS decision. Retrieved from olympics.org/news/ioc-statement-on-cas-decision

IOC. (4 February, 2018b). Request to invite 15 athletes and coaches to PyeongChang 2018. Retrieved from olympics.org/news/request-to-invite-15-athletes-and-coaches-to-pyeongchang-2018-for-the-olympic-athlete-from-russia-group-declined

IOC rep downplays women's hockey party. (26 February, 2010). *CBC News*. Retrieved from cbc.ca/olympics/hockey/story/2010/02/26/sp-hockey-women-drinking-html

ISBF. (19 December, 2017). ISBF Executive Committee will challenge Hearing Panel decision. Retrieved from isbf.org/en/news/20410-ibsf-executive-committee-will-challenge-hearing-panel-decision-against-provisional-suspension-in-front-of-cas

ISLJ Conference. (20 November, 2017). Keynote discussion between Michael Beloff and Sean Cottrell. Retrieved from asser.nl/SportsLaw/Blog/post/example_of_post_with_islj_video

Jakobsson, J., et al. (2006). Large differences in testosterone excretion in Korean and Swedish men. *Journal of Clinical Endocrinology & Metabolism*, 91(2), 687–693.

Jaratt, I. (January 1995). The ten worst performances of 1994. *Inside Sport*. p.26.

Jedlicka, S. (2014). The normative discourse of anti-doping policy. *International Journal of Sport Policy and Politics*, 6(3), 429–444.

Johnson, T., & Skelton, J. (2016). Who really brings the game into disrepute? *Swaab Attorneys*. Retrieved from schwaab.com.au/Publications/Publications/Who-really-brings-the-game-into-disrepute

Jonson, P., Lynch, S., & Adair, D. The contractual and ethical duty for a professional athlete to be an exemplary role model. *Australian and New Zealand Sports Law Journal*, 8(1), 55–88.

Judicial review of international arbitral awards. (29 July, 2010). Swiss International Arbitration Decisions. Retrieved from swissarbitrationdecisions.com/judicial-review-of-international-arbitral-awards-limited-by-art-

Kanagaratnam, S. (2016). Issues in the gathering and use of non-analytical evidence to prove anti-doping rule violations. In Haas & Healey (Eds.), *Sport, Drugs and the Law* (pp. 107–26).

Kane, D. (2003). Twenty years on: An evaluation of the Court of Arbitration for Sport. *Melbourne Journal of International Law*, 4(2), 611–636.

Kaufmann-Kohler, G., & Rigozzi, A. (13 November, 2007). Legal opinion on the conformity of Article 10.6 of the 2007 Draft World Anti-Doping Code with the fundamental rights of athletes. *WADA-AMA*. Retrieved from wada-ama.org/sites/default/files/resources/files/Legal_Opinion_Conformity_10_6_complete_document.pdf

Kelly Sotherton will reject 'dirty and tainted' bronze medal. (26 April, 2017). *The Independent*. Retrieved from independent.co.uk/sport/Olympics/kelly-sotherton-rejects-bronze-medal-russian-drugs-cheat-tatyana-chernova-a7702371.html

Kelner, M. (24 October, 2017). UK Sport may hit British Para-Swimmng in pocket over bullying crisis. *The Guardian*.

theguardian.com/sport/2017/oct/24/uk-sport-british-para-swimming-bullying-crisis-chris-furber

Kim, H. (4 February, 2018). 'IOC chief calls CAS decision "extremely disappointing"' *AP News*. Retrieved from apnews.com/de27309a0cf6407aaebd70b55d30d010

Kolata, G. (30 April, 2008). Some athletes' genes help outwit doping test. *New York Times*. nytimes.com/2008/04/30/sports/30doping.html

Kosla, M. (2001). Disciplined for 'bringing a sport into disrepute' – a framework for judicial review. *Melbourne University Law Review*, *25*(3), 654–679.

Lee, C. (2017). How the Foreign Corrupt Practices Act can help referee FIFA. *Maryland Journal of International Law*, *31*(1), 283–310.

Legal Aid Ontario. (2016). *Government of Ontario*. Retrieved from legalaidontario.ca

Lenskyj, H. (1998). 'Inside Sport' or 'on the margins'? Australian women and the sport media. *International Review for the Sociology of Sport*, *33*(1), 19–32.

Lenskyj, H. (2000). *Inside the Olympic Industry: Power, Politics and Activism*. Albany, NY: SUNY Press.

Lenskyj, H. (2002). *The Best Olympics Ever? Social Impacts of Sydney 2000*. Albany, NY: SUNY Press.

Lenskyj, H. (2008). *Olympic Industry Resistance: Challenging Olympic Power and Propaganda*. Albany, NY: SUNY Press.

Lenskyj, H. (2010). Olympic power, Olympic politics: Behind the scenes. In A. Bairner & G. Molnar (Eds.), *The Politics of the Olympics* (pp. 15–26). London: Routledge.

Lenskyj, H. (2013). *Gender Politics and the Olympic Industry*. Houndmills, Hampshire: Palgrave.

Lenskyj, H. (2014). *Sexual Diversity and the 2014 Sochi Olympics: No More Rainbows*. Houndmills, Hampshire: Palgrave.

Lenskyj, H. (2017). Olympic ideals and the limitations of liberal protest. *International Journal of Sport History*, *34*(3–4), 184–200.

Lenskyj, H. (2018). Sport exceptionalism and the Court of Arbitration for Sport. *Journal of Criminological Research, Policy and Practice*, *4*(1), 5–17.

Lenskyj, H., & Wagg, S. (Eds.). (2012). *Palgrave Handbook of Olympic Studies*. Basingstoke: Palgrave Macmillan.

Lindgren, K. (2016). International and domestic arbitration. In M. Legg (Ed.), *Resolving Civil Disputes* (pp. 209–221). Sydney: LexisNexis.

Logan, D. (June 13, 2013). May the best meds win. *Speed Endurance*. Retrieved from speedendurance.com/2013/06/13/shin-splints-redux-may-the-best-meds-win/

Lopez, B. (November 2010). Doping as technology: A re-reading of the history of performance-enhancing substance use. *ICS Occasional Papers*, *1*(4), 1–17.

MacIntyre, I. (23 November, 2010). For Jon Montgomery, both the beer and the medal were golden. *Vancouver Sun*. Retrieved from vancouversun.com/sports/Montgomery+both+beer+medal+were+golden/7596728/story.html

Maisonneuve, M. (2016). Oberlandesgericht Munchen Az. U. 1110/14 Kart, Claudia Pechstein v/International Skating Union (ISU), 15 January 2015. In A. Duval & A. Rigozzi

(Eds.), *Yearbook of International Sports Arbitration 2015* (pp. 335–348). The Hague: Asser Press.

Major breakthrough in the fight against doping. (1993). *Olympic Review*, No.309–10, 298–300.

Mangan, M. (2009). The Court of Arbitration for Sport: Current practice, emerging trends and future hurdles. *Arbitration International*, 25(4), 591–602.

Mavromati, D. (2016). The legality of the arbitration agreement in favour of CAS under German civil and competition law. *TAS/CAS Bulletin*, 27–60.

Mazanov, J. (2016). *Managing Drugs in Sport* (pp. 175–194). London: Routledge.

Mazzucco, M., & Findlay, H. (2010). Re-thinking the legal regulation of the Olympic regime. In R. Barney, J. Forsyth, & R. Heine (Eds.), *Rethinking Matters Olympic* (pp. 363–375). International Centre for Olympic Research, University of Western Ontario.

M'Baye, K. (1983, November). The Court of Arbitration for Sport. *Olympic Review*, 193, 761–763.

McArdle, D. (2011). Longitudinal profiling, sports arbitration and the woman who had nothing to lose. In M. McNamee & V. Moller (Eds.), *Doping and Anti-Doping Policy in Sport* (pp. 50–65). London: Routledge.

McArdle, D. (2013). CAS 2009/A/1912–1913 *Pechstein v International Skating* Union. In J. Anderson (Ed.), *Leading Cases in Sports Law* (pp. 209–228). The Hague: Asser.

McArdle, D. (2015). *Dispute Resolution in Sport*. London: Routledge.

McArdle, D., & Callery, C. (2011). Doping, European law and the implications of Meca-Medina. *International Journal of Sports Policy and Politics, 3*(2), 163–174.

McLaren, R. (1998). A new order: Athletes' rights and the Court of Arbitration for Sport. *Olympika, VII,* 1–23.

McLaren, R. (2001a). Introducing the Court of Arbitration for Sport: The Ad Hoc Division at the Olympic Games. *Marquette Sports Law Review, 12*(1), 515–544.

McLaren, R. (2001b). Sports law arbitration by CAS: Is it the same as international arbitration? *Pepperdine Law Review, 29*(1), 101–115.

McLaren, R. (2001c). The Court of Arbitration for Sport: An independent arena for the world's sport disputes. *Valparaiso University Law Review, 35*(2), 379–398.

McLaren, R. (2010). Twenty-five years of the Court of Arbitration for Sport. *Marquette Sports Law Review, 20*(2), 305–333.

Menkel-Meadow, C. (1985). Portia in a different voice: Speculations on a women's lawyering process. *Berkeley Journal of Gender, Law and Justice, 1*(1), 39–63.

Menkel-Meadow, C. (2012). Women in dispute resolution. *Dispute Resolution Magazine, 18*(3), 4–11.

Menkel-Meadow, C. (2013). Regulation of dispute resolution in the United States of America. In F. Steffek et al. (Eds.), *Regulating Dispute Resolution: ADR and Access to Justice at the Crossroads* (pp. 419–454). Oxford: Hart.

Mestre, A. (2007). The legal basis of the Olympic Charter. *World Sports Law Report, 5*(11), 6–7.

Ministry of Health. (April, 2012). *Gender Reassignment Health Services for Trans People within New Zealand*. Wellington: Ministry of Health. Retrieved from health.gov/ nz/system/files/documents/publications/gender-reassignment-health-services-for-trans-people-in-nz-v3oct14.pdf

Mitten, M. (2014). The Court of Arbitration for Sport and its global jurisprudence. *Ohio State Journal on Dispute Resolution, 30*(1), 1−44.

Mitten, M., & Opie, H. (2012). 'Sports law': Implications for the development of international, comparative and national law and global dispute resolution. In R. Siekmann & J. Soek (Eds.), *Lex Sportiva: What Is Sports Law?* (pp. 173−222). The Hague: ASSER Press.

Moller, V., & Dimeo, P. (2014). Anti-doping − the end of sport. *International Journal of Sport Policy, 6*(2), 259−272.

Morek, R. (2012). Everyone wants to win: Mediation in sport disputes. *Kluwer Mediation Blog*. Retrieved from mediate.com/articles/MorekRbl20120611.cfm

Moses, M. (2008). *The Principles and Practices of International Commercial Arbitration* (2nd ed.). Cambridge: Cambridge University Press.

Munro, B. (2016). Sport as a force for good. In G. Sweeney (Ed.), *Transparency International: Global Corruption Report* (pp. 3−11). London: Routledge.

Murphy, J. (24 April, 2013). Where in the world is doping a crime? *FlagPost Parliamentary Library of Australia*. Retrieved from aph.gov.au/About_Parliamentary/ Parliamentary_Departments/Parliamentary_Library/FlagPost/ 2013/April/where_in_the_world_is_doping_a_crime_doping_ in_sports_pt_6

Nader, L. (1993). Controlling processes in the practice of law. *Ohio State Journal on Dispute Resolution*, 9(1), 1–26.

Nafziger, J. (2006). The future of international sports law. *Willamette Law Review*, 42(4), 861–875.

Nehme, M., & Ordway, C. (2016). Governance and anti-doping. In Haas & Healey (Eds.), *Sport, Drugs and the Law* (pp. 207–32).

Netzle, S. (1992). The Court of Arbitration for Sport. *Entertainment and Sports Lawyer*, 10(1), 1–9.

Noakes, T. (31 August, 2011). Too fast to be a woman. *The Passionate Eye*, directed by M. Ginnane, CBC Television.

Ordway, C., & Opie, H. (2017). Integrity and corruption in sport. In N. Schulenkorf & S. Frawley (Eds.), *Critical Issues in Global Sport Management* (pp. 38–63). London: Routledge.

Oschutz, F. (2002). Harmonization of anti-doping code through arbitration. *Marquette Sports Law Review*, 12(2), 675–702.

O'Toole, M., & Douglas, P. (1988). Fitness: Definitions and development. In M. Shangold & G. Mirkin (Eds.), *Women and Exercise: Physiology and Sports Medicine*. Philadelphia: Davis.

Overbye, M., Knudsen, M., & Pfister, G. (2013). To dope or not to dope: Elite athletes' perceptions of doping deterrents and incentives. *Performance Enhancement and Health*, 2(3), 119–134.

Palmer, J. (30 April, 2012). BOA showed 'colonial arrogance', says Chambers' agent. *UK Reuters*. Retrieved from uk.reuters.com/article/olympics-doping-chambers/boa-

showed-colonial-arrogance-says-chambers-agent-
idINDEE83T0H320120430

Parry, J. (2006). Doping in the UK: Alain and Dwayne, Rio
and Greg — not guilty? *Sport in Society*, *9*(2), 269–296.

Paulsson, J. (2016). Assessing the usefulness and legitimacy
of CAS. In A. Duval & A. Rigozzi (Eds.), *Yearbook of
International Sports Arbitration 2015* (pp. 3–15). The
Hague: Asser Press.

Pavitt, M. (30 September, 2017). No need for crackdown on
athletes' freedom despite evening exploits. *Inside the Games*.
Retrieved from insidethegames.biz/articles/1056003/michael-
pavitt-no-need-for-crackdown-on-athletes-freedom-despite-
evening-exploits

Peacock, B. (2010). 'A virtual world government unto itself':
Uncovering the rational-legal authority of the IOC in world
politics. In R. Barney, J. Forsyth, & R. Heine (Eds.),
Rethinking Matters Olympic (pp. 318–333) International
Centre for Olympic Research, University of Western Ontario.

Pielke, R. (24 August, 2017). Inconsistencies between Johaug
vs. Sharapova at CAS. *The Least Thing Blog*. Retrieved from
leastthing.blogspot.ca/2017/08/inconsistencies-between-
johaug-vs.html

Pilger, J. (8 August, 2012). How the chosen ones ended
Australia's sporting prowess and revealed its secret past. *New
Statesman*. Retrieved from newstatesman.com/politics/
politics/2012/08/john-pilger-how-the-chosen-ones-ended-
australia's-sporting-prowess-and-reveale

Play the Game. (8 June, 2017). One in seven Olympic
committees are directly linked to governments. Retrieved

from playthegame.org/news/news-articles/2017/0311_one-in-seven-olympic-committees-are-directly-linked-to-governments

Powell, M. (August 8, 2017). Justin Gatlin is an athlete of his time, not a villain. *New York Times*. Retrieved from nytimes.com.2017/08/08/sports/justin-gatlin-doping.html?_r=0

Reeb, M. (2010). The new code of sports-related arbitration. *TAS/CAS Bulletin*. Retrieved from tas-cas.org/fileadmin/user_upload/Bulletin01112010.pdf

Reilly, L. (2012). Introduction to the Court of Arbitration for Sport (CAS) & the role of national courts in international sports disputes. *Journal of Dispute Resolution*, 1(5), 63–81.

Rickenlund, A., et al. (2003). Hyperandrogenicity is an alternative mechanism underlying oligomenorrhea or amenorrhea in female athletes and may improve physical performance. *Fertility and Sterility*, 79(4), 945–955.

Rigozzi, A. (2010). Challenging awards of the Court of Arbitration for Sport. *Journal of International Dispute Settlement*, 1(1), 217–265.

Rigozzi, A., Besson, S., & McAuliffe, W. (2016). International sports arbitration. *European, Middle Eastern and African Arbitration Review* (pp. 1–7). UK: Global Arbitration Review.

Rigozzi, A., Viret, M., & Wisnosky, E. (11 November, 2013). Does the World Anti-Doping Code revision live up to its promises? *Jusletter*. Retrieved from papers.ssm.com/so13/papers.cfm?abstract_id=2411990

Rigozzi, A., Viret, M., & Wisnosky, E. (21 March, 2014). Latest changes to the 2015 WADA Code. *Jusletter*. Retrieved from papers.ssm.com/so13/papers.cfm?abstract_id=2412012

Ritchie, I. (2013). The construction of a policy: The World Anti-Doping Code's 'spirit of sport' clause. *Performance Enhancement and Health*, 2(4), 194–200.

Ritzen, M., et al. (2015). Letter to the Editor. *Journal of Clinical Endocrinology & Metabolism*, 82(2), 307.

Robinson, N., et al. (2012). 2011 IAAF World Championships in Daegu. *Bioanalysis*, 4(13), 1633–1643.

Ruiz, R. (22 April, 2016a). Swiss city is the 'Silicon valley' of sports. *New York Times*. Retrieved from nytimes.com/2016/04/23/sports/olympics/switzerland-global-sports-capital-seeks-new-recruits.html?_r=1

Ruiz, R. (7 June, 2016b). Sport arbitration court ruling against German speedskater Claudia Pechstein is upheld. *New York Times*. Retrieved from nytimes.com/2016/06/08/sports/sports-arbitration-court-ruling-against-german-speedskater-claudia-pechstein-is-upheld.html

Russian deputy prime minister questions testing method for doping substance turinabol. *TASS Russian News Agency* Retrieved from tass.com/sport/942450

Sack, A., & Staurowsky, E. (1998). *College Athletes for Hire: The Evolution and Legacy of the NCAA's Amateur Myth*. Santa Barbara, CA: Praeger.

Samaranch, J. (March/April, 1994). Speech of H.E. Juan Antonio Samaranch, IOC President. *Olympic Review, 316*, 63–65.

Santner, S. et al. (1998). Comparative rates of androgen production and metabolism is Caucasian and Chinese subjects. *Journal of Clinical Endocrinology & Metabolism*, 83(6), 2104–2109.

Saunders, J., & Partridge, J. (25 January, 1999). Toronto bid may profit from Olympic Games scandal, *Globe and Mail*, S2.

Savulescu, J., Foddy, B., & Clayton, M. (2004). Why we should allow performance enhancing drugs in sport. *British Journal of Sports Medicine, 38*(6), 666–670.

Schneider, A. (2004). Privacy, confidentiality and human rights in sport. *Sport in Society, 7*(3), 438–456.

Schrotenboer, B. (28 November, 2017). Judge partly allows Lance Armstrong doping defense at trial. *USA Today*. Retrieved from usatoday.com/story/sports/2017/11/28/judge-partly-allows-lance-armstrong-doping-defense-trial/904110001

Schultz, J. (2012). Disciplining sex: 'Gender verification' policies and women's sport. In H. Lenskyj & S. Wagg (Eds.), *Palgrave Handbook of Olympic Studies* (pp. 410–460). Houndmills, Hampshire: Palgrave.

Schulze, J., et al. (2008). Doping test results dependent on genotype of uridine diphospho-glucuronosyl transferase 2B17. *Journal of Clinical Endocrinology & Metabolism, 93*(7), 2500–2506.

Schwaar, G. (July/August, 1993). Court of Arbitration for Sport. *Olympic Review, 309*, 305–306.

Schwab, B. (3 March, 2013). *ABC Radio: The Ticket*. Retrieved from abc.net.au/news/2013-03-02/jailing-doping-athletes-draconian-and-ridiculous/454927

Setting aside an award for violation of public policy (principle of res judicata). (13 April, 2010). *Swiss International Arbitration Decisions*. Retrieved from swissarbitrationdecisions.com/setting-aside-an-award-for-violation-of-public-policy-principle

Skinner, J. (12 November, 2017). Swim coach Scott Volkers, charged with indecent treatment of a child, *ABC News*. Retrieved from abc.net.au/2017-11-13/swim-coach-scott-volkers-allowed-to-keep-passport-court-rules/9143732

Smith, A., & Stewart, B. (2015). Why the war on drugs in sport will never be won. *Harm Reduction Journal*, *12*(1), 53–59.

Sonksen, P., et al. (2015a). Authors' response to letter by Ritzen et al. *Journal of Clinical Endocrinology & Metabolism*, *82*(2), 308–309.

Sonksen, P., et al. (2015b). Medical and ethical concerns regarding women with hyperandrogenism and elite sport. *Journal of Clinical Endocrinology & Metabolism*, *100*(3), 825–827.

Spera, S. (31 January, 2017). Time for transparency at the Court of Arbitration for Sport. *Asser International Sports Law Blog*, Retrieved from asser.nl/SportsLaw/Blog/post/transparency-at-the-court-of-arbitration-for-sport-by-saveriospera

Strahm, E., et al. (2009). Steroid profiles of professional soccer players: An international comparative study. *British Sports Medicine Journal*, *43*(14), 1126–1130.

Straubel, M. (2005). Enhancing the performance of the doping court: How the Court of Arbitration for Sport can do its job better. *Loyola University Chicago Law Journal*, *36*(4), 1203–1272.

Stringer, H. (January 1995). China's Great Wall of lies. *Inside Sport*, 14–23.

Suchet, A., Jorand, D., & Tuppen, J. (2010). History and geography of a forgotten Olympic project: The Spring Games. *Sport in History*, *30*(4), 570–587.

TAS-CAS. (2012). Code: Statutes of ICAS and CAS. Retrieved from tas-cas.org/fileadmin/user_upload/Code20201220_en_2001.01.pdf

TAS-CAS. (2013). Legal aid. Retrieved from tas-cas.org/en/arbitration/legal-aid.html

TAS-CAS. (18 November, 2014). Governing body of the Court of Arbitration for Sport announces new members. Retrieved from tas-cas.org/fileadmin/user_upload/Media_Release_ICAS_Nov_2014_FINAL.pdf

TAS-CAS. (2016a). Code: Statutes of ICAS and CAS. Retrieved from tas-cas.org/en/icas-code-statutes-of-icas-and-cas.html

TAS-CAS. (2016b). Statistiques/Statistics. Retrieved from tas-cas.org.fileadmin/user_upload/CAS_statistics_2016.pdf

TAS-CAS. (1 January, 2017a). Amendments to the Code of Sports-related Arbitration. Retrieved from tas-cas.org/fileadmin/user/user_upload/Amendments_Code_2017_tracked_changes.pdf

TAS-CAS. (19 January, 2017b). ICAS, the governing body of the Court of Arbitration for Sport, appoints additional arbitrators and mediators. Retrieved from tas-cas.org/en/media/media-releases.html

TAS-CAS. (2017c). Code: Statutes of ICAS and CAS, procedural rules. Retrieved from tas-cas.org/en/arbitration/code-procedural-rules.html

TAS-CAS. (19 April, 2017d). Biathlon – Anti-doping.
Retrieved from tas-cas.org/fileadmin/user_upload/Media_
Release_4889.pdf

TAS-CAS. (4 January, 2018a). Anti-doping – bobsleigh/
skeleton – Russia. Retrieved from tas-cas.org/fileadmin/user/
user_upload/Media_Release_5476.pdf

TAS-CAS. (19 January, 2018b). Athletics: Dutee Chand.
Retrieved from tas-cas.org/Release,tas-cas.org/fileadmin/user_
upload/Media_Release_3759_Jan_2018.pdf

TAS-CAS. (1 February, 2018c). Anti-doping – Sochi 2014.
Retrieved from cas.org/fileadmin/user_upload/Media_
Release_hearing_RUS_IOC_FINAL.pdf

Teetzel, S. (2006). Equality, equity, and inclusion: Issues in
women and transgendered athletes' participation at the
Olympics. In N. Crowther, M. Heine, & R. Barney (Eds.),
*Cultural Imperialism in Action: Critiques in the Global
Olympic Trust, International Centre for Olympic Research*
(pp. 331–338). London: University of Western Ontario.

Tyson Fury says he wants to become a people's champion.
(28 November, 2017). *BBC*. bbc.com/sport/boxing/
42154202

Ulrich, R. et al. (2018). Doping in two elite athletics
competitions assessed by randomized-response surveys.
Sports Medicine, *48*(1), 211–219.

Valloni, L. (9 April, 2012). The Pechstein decision – the end
of sports jurisdiction as we know it? *Sports and Taxation*.
Retrieved from sportsandtaxation.com/2015/04/the-pechstein-
decision-the-end-of-sports-jurisdiction-as-we-know-it/

Valloni, L., & Pachmann, T. (July 25, 2012). Switzerland:
The landmark Matuzalem case and its consequences on the

FIFA regulations. *Mondaq Law*. Retrieved from mondaq. com/x/184712/Sport/The+Landmark+Matuzalem+Case+And +Its+Consequences+On+The+FIFA

van Luikj, N. (2017). The IOC and the United Nations: Strategic and strange bedfellows? Retrieved from cszto. blogspot.ca/2017/05/the-ioc-and-united-nations-strategic. html

Vella, S. (1989). Re *Blainey and Ontario Hockey Association*: Removal of 'No female athletes allowed' signs in Ontario. *Canadian Journal of Women and the Law*, *3*(2), 634–643.

Victorian Equal Opportunity and Human Rights Commission. (2010). Equal Opportunity Act 2010 – Section 72 Exception. Retrieved from austlii.edu.au/ cgi-bin/viewdoc/au/legia/vic/consol_act/eoa2010250/ s72.html

WADA. (2004). WADA technical document – TD2004EEAS. *WADA-AMA*. Retrieved from wada-ama.org/ sites/default/files/resources/files/WADA-TD2004-EAAS-Reporting-and-Evaluation-Guidance-for-Testosterone%2C-Epitestosterone%2C-T-E-Ratio-and-Other-Endogenous-Steroids.pdf

WADA. (2015). World anti-doping code. *WADA-AMA*. Retrieved from wada-ama.org/sites/default/files/resources/ files/wada-2015-world-anti-doping-code.pdf

WADA. (2 April, 2017a). WADA statement on ARD documentary. *WADA-ADA*. Retrieved from wada-ama.org/ en/media/news/2017-04/wada-statement-on-ard-documentary

WADA. (3 April, 2017b). WADA publishes 2015 anti-doping rule violations report. *WADA-AMA*. Retrieved from wada-ama.org/en/media/news/2017-04/wada-publishes-2015-anti-doping-rule-violations-report

WADA. (2017c). Athlete biological passport. *WADA-AMA*. Retrieved from wada-ama.org/en/athlete-biological-passport

WADA. (1 January, 2018a). Summary of major modifications and explanatory notes. *WADA-ADA*. Retrieved from wada-ama.org/sites/default/files/prohibited_list_2018_summary_of_modifications_en.pdf

WADA. (1 February, 2018b). WADA statement regarding CAS decisions. *WADA-ADA*. Retrieved from ama.org/en/media/news/2018-02/wada-statement-regarding-cas-decisions-in-the-matterof-39-russian-athletes

WADC Commentary Team. (November, 2017a). The Johaug CAS award: Too harsh? *WADC Commentary*. wadc.commentary.com/Johaug/

WADC Commentary Team. (November, 2017b). The significance of Maria Sharapova's fault. *WADC Commentary*. Retrieved from wadc.commentary.com/sharapova_cas/

Wendt, J. (2012). Drug testing through the lens of a member of the Court of Arbitration for Sport. *Journal of Legal Aspects of Sport*, *29*(2), 179–185.

Wolf, K. (2014). The non-existence of private self-regulation in the transnational sphere and its implications for the responsibility to procure legitimacy: The case of the lex sportiva. *Global Constitutionalism*, *3*(3), 275–309.

World Anti-Doping Agency figures show 14% rise in doping sanctions. (4 April, 2017). *BBC Sport*. bbc.sport/39486028

World Players Association. (2017). Universal Declaration of Player Rights. Retrieved from uniglobalunion.org/sites/default/files/imce/world_players_udpr_1_page_0.pdf

Young, M. (2010). The IOC made me do it: Women's ski jumping, VANOC and the 2010 Winter Olympics. *Constitutional Forum*, *18*(3), 95–107.

INDEX